Bookpeople

BOOKPEOPLE
A Multicultural Album

Sharron L. McElmeel
Drawings by Deborah L. McElmeel

1992
TEACHER IDEAS PRESS
A Division of
Libraries Unlimited, Inc.
Englewood, Colorado

TEACHER IDEAS PRESS
A Division of
Libraries Unlimited, Inc.
P.O. Box 6633
Englewood, CO 80155-6633

Library of Congress Cataloging-in-Publication Data

McElmeel, Sharron L.
    Bookpeople : a multicultural album / Sharron L. McElmeel ; drawings by Deborah L. McElmeel.
    xvii, 170 p. 22x28 cm.
    Includes bibliographical references and index.
    ISBN 0-87287-953-4
    1. Children's literature--Bio-bibliography. 2. Authors--20th century--Biography. 3. Authors, American--20th century--Biography. 4. Pluralism (Social sciences) 5. Pluralism (Social sciences)--United States. 6. United States--Ethnic relations. 7. United States--Race relations. I. Title. II. Title: Book people.
PN497.M34 1992
809'.89282--dc20
[B]
                                                  92-13252
                                                      CIP

For   *E. J.*
Michael
Deborah
Thomas
Matthew
Steven
Suzanne

because they are still forevermore and always.

Contents

Acknowledgments

In the acknowledgments to *An Author a Month (for Nickels)*, I quoted Tony Johnston, who said, "I write because I would rather not iron." She writes because she must, because she loves it. And I share those sentiments. Things have not changed in my household: I'd still rather write than iron, or for that matter, cook, clean, or do windows. My family makes it possible for me to do the things I like doing best. They also help file and reshelve—Suzanne, especially, who organizes and keeps tabs on my schedule and family appointments. This book would not have been written without my family's support. A special thanks to each of them. And as my "at-home" family dwindles, I recognize even more their contributions to my life.

The inspiration and encouragement to compile information about the people who create books comes from my professional colleagues, who tell wonderful stories of their young students' interest in knowing more. This multicultural volume of bookpeople is motivated by some special young people in my life, Mick, Jade, and Aubrey. As I have searched for books that will reflect Mick and Jade's Native-American heritage, I became painfully aware of how few books there are that reflect their Native American culture and the cultures of other minorities. Aubrey will have little difficulty finding books that reflect her heritage, but she, too, needs to understand that various cultures and people are a vital part of our society. This book was written to contribute to their understanding and to that of many other children (and adults).

I especially appreciate the cooperation of the subjects of this book, and I wish to thank the editors, publicists, marketing directors, and others at the publishing houses who helped me connect with these authors and illustrators, especially Noriko Ichikawa, Dowa-Ya; Heather Zousmer, Random House; David E. Des Jardines, Penguin USA; Sarah Shealy, Harcourt Brace Jovanovich; Emily Widmann, Scholastic; Elinor Young and William C. Morris, HarperCollins; Jessica Franks and Susan George, Bantam; Bruce Lyons, Macmillan/Bradbury; and Marina Tristán, Arte Publico Press. Once again I must extend my thanks and appreciation to the staff of the reference department and the children's services division of the Cedar Rapids (Iowa) Public Library. They have helped verify dates and information and locate books and facts, and they have done so with immeasurable patience and professionalism. For her inspiration and enthusiasm for good books, my thanks to Nancy Jennings of the O. G. Waffle Bookhouse in Marion, Iowa. In addition to her constant encouragement and validation of my efforts, I must extend my appreciation and special thanks to Carolyn Horton for her professional and personal support, advice, and companionship.

Introduction

Our students need to confront the diverse cultural heritages of the world's many peoples, and they need to know the origins and evolution of the political, religious, and social ideas that have shaped our institutions and others.[1]

—Bradley Commission on History in the Schools

Multicultural understanding and appreciation must become an integral part of classroom and library media center instruction, and literature plays a vital role in this process. Studies indicate that to foster positive self-image in all students, educators must seek out and use on a daily basis books that promote multicultural awareness, books that reflect the people, lifestyles, values, and beliefs of a variety of cultural groups.[2] Authors and illustrators, as well as educators, are concerned about images projected in books, especially when most books depict or tell stories only about members of the predominant culture. Children of all races must be able to identify favorite literary characters from many different cultures. Concerns about the inclusion and portrayal of minority cultures and the cultures of other nations must be reflected in the development of regular curriculum units; contributions of authors and illustrators whose works reflect these cultures must not be ignored or relegated only to special focus weeks or months.

This book presents suggestions for integrating literature and multicultural awareness into classroom and library media center activities. *Bookpeople: A Multicultural Album* features fifteen creators of books for children and young people. Each section includes an author/illustrator photograph page and a large-print page containing basic information about that person. Additional sections provide more details about each bookperson's life and work and present summaries and response suggestions (activities) for a selection of that bookperson's work. The activity sessions will promote growth in students' ability to read, think critically, write, and express ideas through a variety of channels, including oral and visual communication. In addition to providing a breathing space between books, these response suggestions also encourage interaction among children and present an opportunity to reflect upon a book and its meaning.

One structure for integrating literature into the curriculum—a structure that has worked well within many literature-based classrooms—is the author focus. Concentrating on the books of one author/illustrator builds respect for that person's work, helps readers make connections, and makes the entire library a reading source as children search for more of the bookperson's work and for connecting themes. The author focus can provide a starting point for reading and sharing books that represent many experiences and a variety of cultures. Where the bookperson represents a culture or heritage unfamiliar to the reader, the author focus helps develop an understanding and appreciation of that heritage or culture. Those readers who are of the culture represented by the bookperson will find their heritage validated, and many, in fact, gain new insight into their own cultural background.

---

[1]Bradley Commission on History in the Schools, *Building a History Curriculum: Guidelines for Teaching History in Schools* (Washington, D.C.: National Institute of Education, Department of Education, 1983). Copies of this report are available from the Educational Excellence Network, 1112 Sixteenth Street NW, Suite 500, Washington, DC 20036. Cost is $3 per copy.

[2]Nancy Larrick, "All-White World of Children's Books," 48 *Saturday Review* 1965, 63-65, 84-85; D. Muse, "Black Children's Literature: Rebirth of a Neglected Genre," *Black Scholar* volume 7, 1965, 11-15; P. Cornelius, "Interracial Children's Books: Problems and Progress," 41 *Library Quarterly* 1971, 106-27; Rudine Sims, *Shadow and Substance: Afro-American Experiences in Contemporary Children's Fiction*, Urbana, Ill.: National Council of Teachers of English, 1982.

Some of my colleagues follow the "author-a-month" timetable, focusing on one author/illustrator per month. Others use the same concept but vary the time spent on each bookperson. The author chosen is suggested by the goals of the curriculum already being studied, and each focus will lead to the reading of works by other authors on similar or contrasting themes.

When an author focus is used in the classroom or library media center, an author center displaying all of the books by that bookperson can be set up in the media center or classroom. A schoolwide or multiple-classroom focus must be organized a little differently: each classroom and the library should have an author center featuring the selected author/illustrator. Books should be in the library on reserve for children to read independently. Individual titles may be checked out by the teacher for a classroom activity dealing with a specific book title. When the activity is finished, the title is returned to the library for others to use and read. It is helpful if multiple copies of books can be available. If possible, keep one copy in a reading area in the library and allow the second copy of the title to circulate to classrooms. During the author focus, the teacher or library media specialist should read aloud many works by the bookperson. It is not intended, however, that all books suggested be used in any one classroom, nor will all the response suggestions be utilized. The idea is to select wisely.

In preparing an author focus, the author photograph page and the large-print author information page can be duplicated and used as poster pages to help create a bulletin-board or author center display introducing the featured bookperson. Mount the photocopies to the inside of a file folder. Add some color, using an edging or small, colored illustrations from a periodical or publisher's catalog, and laminate the open folder. Enlarge pictures of book characters onto manila or white oaktag, using an opaque projector or an overhead projector. Trace, add color, and laminate. With each new author focus, be sure to use a map to locate all the geographical settings discussed in the author biography or the books themselves. Use standard reference materials to further highlight the featured culture.

The sections providing more detailed information about author/illustrators can be used as part of the general author focus introduction, or they may be presented when specific books are read and shared. Each focus should culminate in a special response session that involves the whole class and celebrates the bookperson's overall contribution. A group discussion encourages young readers to connect biographical information with the bookperson's work and with the books of other authors/illustrators. Other culminating activities might include declaring an official day in honor of the bookperson, staging a puppet play, or holding a special literary lunch or a special hour simply reading books. Make each activity unique.

Author focuses based on author/illustrators featured in *Bookpeople: A Multicultural Album* have applications to many areas of the curriculum across the grade levels, from kindergarten to middle school. For example, when elementary/middle school language arts classrooms study poetry, the work of Virginia Driving Hawk Sneve could be read. In conjunction with her poetry, information about her Native-American heritage and personal background could be shared, thus providing a role model for Native-American students and creating an awareness of some aspects of Native-American culture for all students. Classes studying the culture of the American South or the sorrow of slavery might be introduced to Julius Lester, a contemporary African-American author who has retold some of the Uncle Remus tales and written dramatic accounts of African Americans caught in the web of slavery. For intermediate/middle school students, Lester's books will be appropriate as independent reading material. Younger students might be introduced to his work through read-alouds. Response suggestions for sharing his books can be adapted for various age groups. A study of Australia would suggest an author focus on Mem Fox, who shares information about her country in her writings. Her books will help build schematic background for primary students and provide a starting point for further investigation for intermediate/middle school students.

My search for authors and illustrators to feature in this multicultural volume turned up several bookpeople who presented an authentic image of African Americans, but the number was not overwhelming; I was only able to identify a few Asian-American authors, two Native Americans, and one Hispanic bookperson. In selecting author/illustrators, I considered a number of criteria. First, the bookperson had to have published more than one book, and these books had to be available through conventional publishing channels. If out of print, these titles had to be relatively available in established libraries and media centers. A further consideration was that the work of these authors and illustrators could be used with a wide variety of grade levels.

The question arose as to whether the book should include only bookpeople who are members of the culture about which they write or illustrate. Such guidelines would have eliminated Paul Goble, an Englishman whom many consider the premier author/illustrator now writing children's literature about Native Americans. And what about authors and illustrators who are members of minority or foreign cultures but do not treat that culture in their work? This criterion would have eliminated illustrator Donald Crews, an African American, who is an admirable role model but who does not create books about African Americans. The decision I arrived at was to include authors and illustrators who were part of a minority culture or whose writing authentically depicted a minority culture. A related concern was whether to include bookpeople whose work promoted multicultural awareness because it was set in a foreign country. Because part of our understanding of the world involves understanding the cultures of other countries, I decided to include an author from Australia and one from Japan.

Another issue I confronted was appropriate terminology for cultural groups. *Native American, native American Indian*, or simply *American Indian* are all terms used by members of that culture or by authorities who write about the group. I settled on *Native American*. A similar situation arose regarding the terms *Black, Afro American*, and *African American*. I found the three terms used almost interchangeably. I found *African American* more current than *Afro American* and so eliminated the latter, but *African American* was not appropriate for describing Black Africans or Blacks living elsewhere in the world. Consequently, I opted to use both *Black* and *African American* somewhat interchangeably, giving consideration to the origin of the stories under discussion.

After compiling a preliminary list of bookpeople, choices were made from that list for balance, interest, and appropriateness to a wide audience. The final list of fifteen authors/illustrators represents a variety of cultures and geographic regions.

AUTHORS SELECTED AND HOW THEY CONNECT TO A MULTICULTURAL FOCUS

Mitsumasa Anno is a resident of Japan. Although his books do not particularly reflect the culture of Japan, he is a role model who will validate the contributions of the Japanese to our culture. Different age groups will appreciate his books on a variety of levels.

Ashley Bryan writes and illustrates books that reflect his African-American heritage. Younger readers will appreciate the picture-book format of his folktales as well as the rhythm and repetition of the language. Older readers will be interested in his collections of stories and spirituals. Various age groups will be interested in his illustrative technique.

Ann Cameron was born and raised in the Midwest, but she writes stories that reflect her experiences in Guatemala and her exposure to people of various cultural backgrounds. Her tales featuring Julian (as well as his sister Gloria and their friends) depict the life of a Black child in a contemporary setting. Children from second to fifth grade will enjoy these stories; younger children will appreciate them if they are read aloud. Older students who need easier reading material will still find these stories interesting.

Donald Crews is an African American. His books will appeal primarily to the picture-book set, but older students may find them interesting because of the suggested responses the books can motivate. For example, the suggested response activity for *Trucks* that involves creating a trucker's log for the journey requires critical thinking and conjecture as well as the actual mechanics of creating the log. This activity is most appropriate for intermediate readers. Crews's brilliant graphics may inspire some artwork from older students.

Pat Cummings is an African-American illustrator and sometimes an author who consistently portrays Black children in her illustrations. The stories she writes and illustrates are contemporary stories of ordinary children engaged in ordinary activities; the characters just happen to be Black. She is one of the few authors/illustrators who do not rely on folk literature or variant tales when portraying African Americans. She has also written a book about illustrators that features at least three other African Americans: Leo Dillon, Tom Feelings, and Jerry Pinkney.

Mem Fox is an Australian author whose works reflect both the differences between and the similarities among cultures. *Possum Magic* brings about an awareness of the foods, animals, and geography of Australia. How many intermediate students do you think know that Tasmania actually exists? The very young student will enjoy hearing *Hattie and the Fox* over and over again; other students will enjoy reading or hearing Fox's other stories.

Paul Goble is an Englishman, but his intense interest in and study of Native Americans has prompted him to write about this culture. Many Native-American authorities have cited Goble's books for their authenticity. His books, often original stories rooted in the traditions of early Native Americans, consistently tell a good story and respect the essence of Native-American beliefs and styles. He has said that his books and paintings give back to Native Americans things that are really theirs. His books, however, are gifts to non-Native Americans who wish to build a better understanding of a rich and meaningful culture whose members lived in harmony with nature.

Jamake Highwater, winner of the Newbery award, writes about Native Americans. Although there is controversy as to whether he is truly of Native-American heritage, most critics agree that his writing has credibility and deals with topics important to Native Americans. His picture book *Moonsong Lullaby* will appeal to younger readers, and *Anpao* will interest the intermediate or older reader.

Julius Lester, an African American, writes compelling stories about slavery and retells favorite folktales. His novels for older readers show clearly the hardships faced daily by those Blacks forced into slavery. His collections of Brer Rabbit tales and other African-American folktales appeal to intermediate readers and are excellent stories to read aloud to younger students.

Patricia McKissack has for many years devoted herself to bringing stories of the African-American heritage she shares to the mainstream of literature. She is best known for her picture books told in folktale form and for her biographies of notable Blacks. Because her books appeal to a wide range of readers (her books include early readers, pictures books, and intermediate- and junior-high-level biographies), she is an appropriate choice for an author focus.

Nicholasa Mohr is of Puerto Rican heritage, and her books reflect this culture. Most of her stories are written for the older intermediate- or middle/junior-high-level reader, but she has written two books, *Felita* and *Going Home*, that appeal to the late primary/early intermediate reader.

Brian Pinkney is an emerging African-American illustrator whose work affirms the place of Black children in all types of stories. His work displays an inventiveness and imagination that will surely place his work on award lists. The books he works on are heavily illustrated and will appeal to primary and intermediate students.

Virginia Driving Hawk Sneve writes books that reflect her Native-American heritage (she is an enrolled member of the Rosebud Sioux). Her novels for intermediate readers tell a story of Native-American youth in the 1960s striving to cope with the modern world while keeping the traditional values of their culture.

Yoshiko Uchida is a Japanese American. Her writing is unique because it brings forward the experience of the Japanese in America. Her own family's incarceration in a "relocation camp" during World War II provides the foundation for some of her stories. She has also retold traditional Japanese folktales.

Laurence Yep brings his Chinese cultural background into some of his stories, although others are just wonderful mystery stories. Yep's books portray the varied experiences of Chinese Americans and highlight the achievements of the Chinese in the United States. Many of the experiences and achievements of characters in his books reflect his own life as a second-generation Chinese in America.

Those who use this book may well feel that the selection of multicultural authors is incomplete; after seeking out other authors and illustrators whose work promotes multicultural awareness, users may say, "This book should have included _____." This was part of my goal. If I have helped educators become more aware of our responsibility to bring information about a variety of cultures into the classroom and if I have piqued their interest in discovering additional multicultural authors, then this book has succeeded.

Some multicultural authors who should not be missed have been featured previously in *An Author a Month (for Nickels)* (Libraries Unlimited, 1990), *An Author a Month (for Pennies)* (Libraries Unlimited, 1988), *Bookpeople: A First Album* and *Bookpeople: A Second Album* (Libraries Unlimited, 1990). Leo Dillon was the first African American to win a Caldecott medal. He did so in two consecutive years, as co-illustrator with his wife, Diane Dillon. Diane Dillon is not African American by heritage, but with her husband Leo has illustrated many books that bring forth an awareness of the Black culture. The medal was awarded to the Dillons in 1976 for *Why Mosquitoes Buzz in People's Ears* by Verna Aardema (Dial, 1975) and in 1977 for *Ashanti to Zulu* by Margaret Musgrove (Dial, 1976). Leo Dillon and Diane Dillon are featured in *Bookpeople: A First Album* (Libraries Unlimited, 1990). The late John Steptoe is another book-person who merits attention. He won wide acclaim for his story of Black children in the inner city and for his retellings of folktales. He received a Caldecott honor award for his illustrations for *The Story of Jumping Mouse: A Native American Legend* (Lothrop, 1984) and *Mufaro's Beautiful Daughters: An African Tale* (Lothrop, 1987). Steptoe is featured in *An Author a Month (for Nickels)* (Libraries Unlimited, 1990).

Read, share, and enjoy!

Mitsumasa Anno

From *Bookpeople: A Multicultural Album* by Sharron L. McElmeel (Libraries Unlimited, Inc., 1992)

Mitsumasa Anno

Japan is Mitsumasa Anno's homeland. He is best known in the United States as Anno. The illustrations in his books are filled with many hidden details. In *Anno's Journey* he has hidden characters from "Sesame Street," Little Red Riding Hood, Pinocchio, and other well-known story characters. Paintings by Renoir, Van Gogh, and Seurat are hidden in his landscapes.

Anno was born March 20, 1926, in a small, historic town, Tsuwano, in the western part of Japan. While other Japanese school children were learning to copy pictures from books, Anno's teacher encouraged him to do creative sketching.

Anno graduated from Yamaguchi College, became an art teacher, and then began creating children's books. His first book was *Topsy-Turvies*, and one of his most recent books is *kitsune ga hirotta Grimm dowa* (The Grimm Tales That the Fox Gathered). Anno and his wife, Midori, have two children — a son, Masaichiro, and a daughter, Seiko. They live "peacefully" in Tokyo, where Anno paints, lectures on art and art history, and continues to create books.

Mitsumasa Anno

ABOUT THE AUTHOR/ILLUSTRATOR

Mitsumasa Anno, known in the United States as Anno, is a children's book artist and illustrator and, in his native Japan, a noted painter and lecturer on art and art history.

Mitsumasa Anno was born on March 20, 1926, to parents who operated a bustling inn in a small town, Tsuwano, in western Japan. As he was growing up, Anno knew he wanted to be a painter. During his childhood, when other schoolchildren learned how to copy pictures from books, Anno's teacher taught his class to create drawings from the imagination. They were encouraged to illustrate the tale of Urashima Taro, who had been to the Sea God's Palace, and to draw what they wanted to be when they grew up. Because the schoolchildren were encouraged to observe the natural world attentively, Anno learned how to sketch and draw directly from nature.

Anno grew up near the town of Tsuwano but went to high school far from his home. He continued to draw and paint and dreamt of becoming an artist. He also thought about being a professional player of *go* (Japanese checkers). But World War II began, and Anno had to serve in the army. Later he went to Paris, where he visited the tomb of Van Gogh and read books by Maurice Escher. It was his experiences in Paris that inspired Anno to make his first picture book, *Topsy-Turvies*.

Anno's books fall into two categories. The first category includes books that are filled with numerical references and optical illusions. For example, in *Anno's Alphabet*, Anno has seemingly rendered normal objects in a normal environment. But a closer look reveals that the objects are not as they first seem: a hatchet handle is part of a tree trunk, a typewriter has only one letter, and a tube of orange paint disappears into an artist's palette. Anno also plays with the concept of scale. In *The King's Flower* (Collins, 1979), a king thinks that his possessions must be bigger and better than anyone else's. The king's toothbrush is so enormous that it takes two carriers to move it. Anno's meticulous drawings bring a sense of normalcy to scenes that would otherwise be totally implausible.

The second category of Anno's work includes wordless "travel" books such as *Anno's Journey, Anno's Britain, Anno's USA*, and others. Throughout these books, Anno, like Maurice Sendak, cleverly hides images and characters that are sometimes well known and sometimes significant only to the author. For example, Judy Taylor, who was an editor at the prestigious British publishing house of Bodley Head, was quite helpful to Anno during the creation of *Anno's Journey*. It is commonly said that she saved Maurice Sendak's life in 1967 by sending him to a hospital when he suffered a heart attack, in appreciation of which Sendak hid Taylor's name in his book *In the Night Kitchen*.[1] Anno, like Sendak, wanted to commemorate Taylor in his book. He did so in *Anno's Journey*, by including Taylor's house among the houses of well-known people such as Arthur Rackham, Kate Greenaway, and William Morris. Anno also includes a drawing of himself in each of his books.

Anno's illustrations are created using watercolors. Each of his journey books is filled with expanses of fields, rivers, towns, castles, country fairs, gardens, and cathedrals. Dozens and dozens of characters populate each illustration, doing everything from running races to fighting duels to throwing tea into the harbor.

In *Anno's Britain*, Anno arrives in the United Kingdom by boat, travels across the countryside, and then departs by boat. During his travels he meets a copper craftsman, a tinker, and Prince Charles and Princess Diana. He visits the Tower of London, the Loch Ness

[1]For a more detailed discussion of Maurice Sendak and his hidden images in books see *My Bag of Book Tricks* by Sharron McElmeel (Englewood, Colo.: Libraries Unlimited, 1989), 177-79.

Monster, Shakespearean characters King Lear and the Merchant of Venice, and storybook characters Peter Pan, Tinkerbell, Alice in Wonderland, Jack and the Giant, Winnie-the-Pooh, and Toad from *The Wind in the Willows*. Anno hides many other famous places, animals, fictional and fairy-tale characters, and craftsmen within the book. In *Anno's USA*, the same format is followed. Anno's boat takes him to Hawaii and then on to the San Francisco Bay area. From there he travels by horseback across the continental United States. Along the way he meets historical figures John Muir, Betsy Ross, and the Wright Brothers, as well as King Kong, Dorothy from *The Wizard of Oz*, Superman, and other fictional characters. He samples historic events such as the Boston Tea Party.

Anno, who is known in Japan as a first-rate painter, is a member of the Japan Artists Association. He is often asked to lecture on art and art history for television. He considers himself a full-time illustrator and works 6 hours a day. In 1984 he was awarded the prestigious Hans Christian Andersen Award for illustration. Of his present life in Japan, where he lives with his wife, Midori Suetsugu; his daughters, Seiko; and his son, Masaichiro, who was coauthor and coillustrator of *Anno's Magical ABC: An Anamorphic Alphabet* and *Anno's Mysterious Multiplying Jar*, Mitsumasa Anno says simply, "I'm living peacefully."

THE BOOKSHELF

Anno, Mitsumasa. **Anno's Aesop: A Book of Fables by Aesop and Mr. Fox.** Orchard, 1989.

Freddy Fox obviously has not seen a book before he finds one, grimy and battered at the edge of the forest. He begs his father to read the book, but it soon becomes obvious that Freddy's father is better at telling the story than he is at reading it. The fables of Aesop can be read on the upper portion of the book's pages while a continuous panel on the lower portion shows the "reading" Mr. Fox is giving the fables. The pictures are deceptive in their simplicity—visual puzzles abound.

1. Before sharing this variation on the Aesop fables, familiarize readers with traditional versions. Consider sharing selections from some of the titles cited in the following list.

Aesop's Fables

Aesop. *Aesop's Fables*. Selected and illustrated by Michael Hague. Henry Holt, 1985.

_____. *Aesop's Fables*. Retold in verse by Tom Paxton. Illustrated by Robert Rayevsky. Greenwillow, 1988.

_____. *Aesop's Fables*. Illustrated by Lisbeth Zwerger. Picture Book, 1989.

_____. *The Caldecott Aesop*. Illustrated by Randolph Caldecott. Doubleday, 1978.

_____. *Once in a Wood: Ten Tales from Aesop*. Adapted and illustrated by Eve Rice. Greenwillow, 1979.

_____. *Twelve Tales from Aesop*. Retold and illustrated by Eric Carle. Putnam, 1980.

Ash, Russell, and Bernard Higton, compilers. *Aesop's Fables: A Classic Illustrated Edition*. Chronicle, 1990.

Clark, Margaret, reteller. *The Best of Aesop's Fables*. Illustrated by Charlotte Voake. Joy Street, 1990.

2. Share other versions that are noted for their humor.

Aesop's Fables: A Touch of Humor

Aesop. *The Exploding Frog and Other Fables from Aesop*. Retold by John McFarland. Illustrated by James Marshall. Little, Brown, 1981.

Ross, Tony. *Foxy Fables*. Illustrated by Tony Ross. Dial, 1986.

3. Read aloud or ask students to read the twenty original fables in Arnold Lobel's *Fables* (Harper, 1980). Use Lobel's fables to inspire the writing of additional "modern" fables.

    a. Discuss with students how Lobel's literary fables fit the definition of a traditional fable. (As defined by *Funk & Wagnalls Standard Dictionary of Folklore, Mythology & Legend* [Funk & Wagnalls, 1949], a fable is "an animal tale with a moral; a short tale in which animals appear as characters, talking and acting like human beings, though usually keeping their animal traits, and having as its purpose the pointing of a moral. The fable consequently has two parts: the narrative which exemplifies the moral, and the statement of the moral often appended in the form of a proverb.")

    b. Have students write some fables of their own.

Anno, Mitsumasa. **Anno's Math Games**. Philomel, 1982 (1987). **Anno's Math Games II**. Philomel, 1990. **Anno's Math Games III**. Philomel, 1991.

These books are filled with important mathematical concepts and motivational activities.

1. Using the section on sets have students create their own pictures of nine objects, choosing eight objects that are related and one that is different. Students should be ready to defend their categorizations.

2. Another section of the book deals with tangrams. Use this section to introduce the idea of creating figures with the basic tangram forms. Follow the introduction to tangrams by reading *Grandfather Tang's Story* by Ann Tompert, illustrated by Robert Andrew Parker (Crown, 1990).

3. Kriss and Kross are two characters that Anno uses throughout his math books to introduce different concepts. In one section, they create a grid. Along the spaces at the top of the grid are common everyday objects such as a bell, a chimney, and rear-view mirrors. Down the side spaces are other common everyday objects such as a suitcase, baby buggy, and tea cup. As a line is drawn down from any one object along the top, it intersects with a line drawn across from one of the objects along the side. At the point of intersection the reader is to draw a new product created from the elements of the two original objects. For example, the lines drawn from the baby buggy and the rear-view mirrors will intersect at a point where the reader would draw a baby buggy with rear-view mirrors. As each of the pairs is combined, a third object is created. Each of these new objects has potential as a viable product for the marketplace. This activity

should encourage divergent thinking and help stimulate students to develop ideas for other new inventions. To further this focus share books about inventors and inventions. Then have your own classroom "Invention Fair." Some of the following titles will help further the theme.

Inventors and Inventions

Aaseng, Nathan. *Better Mousetraps: Product Improvements That Led to Success.* Illustrated with photographs. Lerner, 1990.

Adler, David A. *A Picture Book of Benjamin Franklin.* Illustrated by John Wallner and Alexandra Wallner. Holiday, 1990.

_____. *Thomas Alva Edison: Great Inventor.* Illustrated by Lyle Miller. Holiday, 1990.

Alter, Judith. *Eli Whitney.* Illustrated with photographs. Watts, 1990.

Bender, Lionel. *Invention.* Knopf, 1991 (Eyewitness Books Series)

Berliner, Don. *Before the Wright Brothers.* Illustrated with photographs. Lerner, 1990.

Buranelli, Vincent. *Thomas Alva Edison.* Burdett, 1990.

Caney, Steven. *Steven Caney's Invention Book.* Workman, 1985.

Collins, David R. *Pioneer Plowmaker: A Story about John Deere.* Illustrated by Steve Michaels. Carolrhoda, 1990.

Cooke, David. *Inventions That Made History.* Putnam, 1986.

Cooper, Chris. *How Everyday Things Work.* Facts on File, 1984.

Feldman, Eve B. *Benjamin Franklin: Scientist and Inventor.* Illustrated with photographs. Watts, 1990.

Freedman, Russell. *The Wright Brothers: How They Invented the Airplane.* Illustrated with photographs by Wilbur and Orville Wright. Holiday, 1991.

Jacobs, Daniel. *What Does It Do?: Inventions Then and Now.* Illustrated by Daniel Jacobs. Raintree, 1990.

Murphy, Jim. *Guess Again: More Weird and Wacky Inventions.* Bradbury, 1986.

_____. *Weird and Wacky Inventions.* Crown, 1978.

Parker, Steve. *The Random House Book of How Things Work.* Random, 1990 (1991).

Pelta, Kathy. *Alexander Graham Bell.* Burdett, 1990.

Richards, Norman. *Dreamers and Doers: Inventors Who Changed Our World.* Atheneum, 1984.

Tames, Richard. *The Wright Brothers.* Illustrated with photographs. Watts, 1990.

Taylor, Barbara. *Weekly Reader Presents Be an Inventor.* Harcourt, 1987.

Taylor, Richard L. *The First Flight: The Story of the Wright Brothers.* Illustrated with photographs. Watts, 1990.

Winn, Chris, and Jeremy Beadle. *Rodney Rootle's Grown-Up Grappler and Other Treasures from the Museum of Outlawed Inventions.* Little, Brown, 1982.

Anno, Mitsumasa. **Anno's Britain**. Philomel, 1982. **Anno's Journey**. Philomel, 1978; Sandcastle, 1978. **Anno's Italy**. Philomel, 1980. **Anno's USA**. Philomel, 1983.

Throughout each of the wordless journeys, Anno tells the reader something about each country (or in the case of *Anno's Journey*, about Europe).

1. Have students use the information given at the end of each book to hunt for literary characters and historical events that are presented in each of Anno's books.

2. Have students research a person or event found in one of the books and write a paragraph or two about the person's or event's significance in the history or culture of the country featured.

3. Have students use large pieces of butcher paper, drawing pencils, and crayons or paints to create panoramas of scenes near their school, neighborhood, or family home. Into that scene they should insert some references to people and events significant in the history of their school, neighborhood, or home. Alice Provensen's *The Buck Stops Here: The Presidents of the United States* (HarperCollins, 1990) will give a simpler (but similar in concept) model for incorporating symbols, headlines, episodes, and other material into single illustrations. The Provensen example will be more collage-like, with white space between each of the symbols included in the illustration.

Anno, Mitsumasa. **In Shadowland**. Orchard, 1988.

Alternating pages of color and black-and-white invite readers into Shadowland. A little match girl and a watchman flee their fellow townspeople and go to Shadowland, where the king declares a wedding. Anno illustrates his story with intricate paper cuts, each of which is created from a single piece of paper.

1. Anno's talent shows through in this unique illustrative technique. Paper-cut scenes are traditionally used in many Asian countries, especially China and Japan. Have students compare Anno's paper cuts with those of another illustrator who uses them extensively, Jan Pienkowski. His books include *Christmas* (Knopf, 1984) and *Easter* (Knopf, 1989). Pienkowski is of Polish descent and now lives in England. His paper-cut style, which combines the eighteenth-century art of silhouetting with brilliant color and sumptuous ornamental gilding, is somewhat different from the traditional cuts from the Asian countries.

2. Have students make their own silhouette pictures. Ask them to cut objects from black paper. Have them glue the objects to a solid-colored backing to create a scene.

FURTHER READING

Mitsumasa Anno has also edited *All in a Day* (Philomel, 1986), a book that projects brotherhood and aptly portrays the contrasts and similarities of children in different parts of the world (Australia, Brazil, China, England, Japan, Kenya, the United States, and the U.S.S.R.) through a single 24-hour day. While children in the United States are sleighriding, children in Kenya are watching a flamingo flying into the star-filled night. Eight scenes are part of each double-page spread. Each scene is drawn by a noted illustrator who represents a featured country: Mitsumasa Anno, Raymond Briggs, Ronald Brooks, Gianvittore Calvi, Eric Carle, Zhu Chengliang, Diane Dillon and Leo Dillon, Akiko Hayashi, and Nicolai Popov. A great book to share and discuss with small groups.

Display books by other Japanese artists/authors in the author corner. Authors you will want to showcase are included in the list below.

Japanese Authors and Illustrators

Keiko Kasza — She was born in Japan but now lives in the United States with her husband and two sons.

Keizabura Tejima — He was born in Hokkaido, Japan, in 1935.

Satomi Ichikawa — She was born in Japan but has lived in France for more than 10 years.

Books by these authors and illustrators can be located by using the catalog in your school or public library.

Ashley Bryan

Ashley Bryan

From *Bookpeople: A Multicultural Album* by Sharron L. McElmeel (Libraries Unlimited, Inc., 1992)

Ashley Bryan

Ashley Bryan was born on July 13, 1923, in New York City. His parents had moved there from the Caribbean island of Antigua after World War I. He had three brothers and two sisters.

When Ashley Bryan began making books in kindergarten, he not only wrote and illustrated them, but he bound and distributed them as well. He continued making books as presents for his family and friends throughout his childhood and into his adult life.

Ashley Bryan's earliest childhood memories include hearing his mother sing and seeing the many birds (at one time more than 100) that his father kept in cages on bookshelves of the family's Bronx apartment. Those memories and the love of poetry are reflected in the rhythmic books he has written and illustrated since the early 1970s.

After many years of teaching in New Hampshire, Ashley Bryan now lives year-round in Islesford, Maine, on an island off the coast, where he has spent summers since 1946. He has made several trips to Africa and often travels across the United States to share his stories and favorite poems. When he is at home, he paints during the day and works on his books at night.

Ashley Bryan

ABOUT THE AUTHOR/ILLUSTRATOR

Ashley Bryan grew up in the toughest of New York City neighborhoods. His parents had emigrated to New York City from Antigua, West Indies, shortly after World War I. Bryan and his three brothers and two sisters were all born and raised in the Bronx. Ashley Bryan was born on July 13, 1923. He credits his kindergarten teacher with teaching him the alphabet, and when he illustrated his ABCs she taught him to put a cover on the pages and to stitch through the pages to hold them together. His interest in bookmaking flourished as his sisters and brothers, mother and father, and aunts and uncles all praised his efforts.

After making his alphabet book, Bryan created a number book, and as he learned, he continued to make books filled with stories and poems. He also credits his teachers with teaching him to read poetry dramatically and rhythmically. By the time he was in fourth grade, he had created hundreds of books and continued making books as presents for family and friends.

In 1946, as a student at the Cooper Union Art School in New York, Bryan won a scholarship to paint in Maine. He earned a degree from the Cooper Union Art School that same year. Later, he majored in philosophy at Columbia University, where he received a degree in 1950. After receiving his degree, while Bryan was teaching at Queens College and living in the Bronx, Jean Karl, an editor at Atheneum who had heard about his work, visited his studio. After seeing all his book projects for family and friends, she sent him a contract to do his first book, *Moon, for What Do You Wait?* (Atheneum, 1967), a collection of one-line poems by Indian poet Sir Rabindranaht Tagore, collected by Richard Lewis.

Bryan became an artist-in-residence at Dartmouth College in Hanover, New Hampshire. By 1973 he had been offered a permanent position on the faculty. For more than a decade, he spent the school year living in Hanover and teaching drawing and painting as a professor of art. Each summer he returned to Islesford, Maine, on the island he had fallen in love with during his student days at the Cooper Union Art School. He continued to read and enjoy the poetry of Paul Dunbar and others and to seek stories from the people and places around him. It wasn't long before he began to retell some of his favorite African folk stories. In 1971 he retold five stories in *The Ox of the Wonderful Horns and Other African Folktales*. Bryan is now professor emeritus of art at Dartmouth and lives year-round in Islesford.

Ashley Bryan rewrites each of his books until the rhythm is perfect. He strives for a special relationship between the words, rhythms, and sounds—a relationship that makes each book a rhythmic story or poem for reading aloud. The songs he collects into books are meant to be sung, just as the African Americans from whom he gathered the songs sang them. In appearances before children, he recites poetry by Langston Hughes, Paul Laurence Dunbar, Gwendolyn Brooks, and Eloise Greenfield; he tells stories and uses his recorder to play spirituals. Many of those spirituals have been included in his collections of folk songs sung by African Americans across the United States.

The text of a book determines the technique and medium Bryan will use to illustrate it. He creates roughs from which he works the finished illustrations. He has illustrated all but one of his books. Bryan's friend Fumio Yoshimura illustrated Bryan's retelling of *Sh-Ko and His Eight Wicked Brothers*, a Japanese tale. During an interview in April 1991, Bryan explained how that came about, Bryan said, "My friend Fumio Yoshimura had done extensive brush paintings to Japanese legends. When I saw the large amount of beautiful brush paintings, I asked him if I could retell one small part of the Sh-Ko story. I wanted children to see the Japanese style of brush painting from this fine artist, since books introduce children to the art of the world."

In some books Bryan uses vibrant watercolors; in others he uses block prints. His illustrations for *The Adventures of Aku; Beat the Story Drum, Pum-Pum*; and *Lion and the Ostrich Chicks* are sometimes said to be block prints or silk-screen prints, but they are in fact, paintings. Bryan prefers paintings for his original art work because they reproduce better. He created the illustrations for his volumes of spirituals using linoleum blocks—to emulate the early religious block-printed books. At first he thought he would have to use wood blocks, but the cost of a good hardwood would have been immense, and he would have had difficulty transporting such heavy and bulky material between Dartmouth and Islesford. He settled on unmounted linoleum because it was lighter and much cheaper, would not splinter, and, most importantly, would allow him to achieve the detail and effect he wanted.

Bryan created the art for *The Ox of the Wonderful Horns, The Adventures of Aku,* and *Beat the Story Drum, Pum-Pum* with tempera paints. His tendency to intersperse paintings in red, black, and ochre with black-and-white paintings is shown in the endpapers.

Bryan's family inspired many of his illustrations. His grandmother Sarah came from Antigua for a visit and stayed 20 years in New York before returning. She inspired the illustrations of the grandmother and child for the spiritual "Somebody's Knocking at Your Door," which Bryan included in *I'm Going to Sing: Black American Spirituals, Vol. II.* She also inspired the retelling and illustrations for *The Dancing Granny.* The story is from the Ashanti tradition but was collected in the West Indies. While Bryan's grandmother was in the United States, she often watched her great-grandchildren dancing. Once she caught onto the pattern of their dance, she would join in, build new patterns on theirs, and then outdance the children. Bryan knew that eventually his granny would have to dance with the ultimate of folktale heroes, Anansi. Anansi is the "spider man" of African folklore. Bryan wanted Granny's partner to be worthy of her, so in *The Dancing Granny*, he made Anansi appear charming, slickly dressed, and convincing. Since Bryan wanted the illustrations to present an image of swiftness and grace, he based his three-color illustrations on his study of Japanese brush painting. He was particularly influenced by the work of Hokusai, who filled sketchbooks with scenes from daily life. Bryan also did a lot of drawing from real life—particularly dancers. His own sketchbooks helped when he began to prepare the illustrations for *The Dancing Granny.* He felt that the fluidity of the brush strokes would achieve the illusion of movement he wanted. *The Dancing Granny* fairly whirls off the page as Granny dances through the story.

Each book brings it own images to Bryan. For Mari Evans's *Jim Flying High* (Doubleday, 1979), Bryan created watercolor illustrations in full color. Illustrations touched with tempera are given a patterned stained-glass effect by the narrow white spaces that appear between each of the shapes that form the images. For the Caribbean tale retold by Susan Cooper as *Jethro and the Jumbie* (Atheneum, 1979), Bryan drew from the many pencil sketches he made during visits with relatives in Antigua. His drawings aptly represent the little boy who befriends the Caribbean boogeyman, Jumbie.

Much of what Ashley Bryan shares with young readers in his books reflects his own experiences and the stories he heard as a child. In the April 1991 interview, he said, "I loved poetry and folktales of the world ... still do." That love of poetry and folktales comes through in everything he does. And what has he been working on recently? Ashley Bryan responded, "I'm always working on retelling African folktales."

THE BOOKSHELF

Bryan, Ashley. **The Adventures of Aku; or, How It Came About That We Shall Always See Okra the Cat Lying on a Velvet Cushion, While Okraman the Dog Sleeps among the Ashes.** Atheneum, 1976.

Usually referred to as *The Adventures of Aku*, this tale has several motifs. It is a tale of magic that contains elements from "Aladdin's Lamp" and "Jack and the Beanstalk." The story includes a dull-but-good-hearted son, a long-suffering mother, an unfair trade, a transformed king, a ring that magically grants wishes, a trickster (in this case Anansi, who appears as a combination of man and insect), and animals (a noble cat, Okra, and a dog, Okraman).

1. Read other tales in which Anansi appears and compare the characteristics of the Anansi character. Usually the first line or two presents Anansi's problem — the problem he will attempt to solve. How does the character show that he is a rogue, a trickster? And how does his wit and cleverness help him to prevail?

Anansi Tales

Aardema, Verna. *Behind the Back of the Mountains: Black Folktales from Southern Africa.* Illustrated by Leo Dillon and Diane Dillon. Dial, 1973.

Courlander, Harold, and George Herzog. "Anansi and Nothing Go Hunting for Wives." In *The Cow-Tail Switch and Other West African Stories.* Illustrated by Madye Lee Chastain. Holt, 1947.

Haley, Gail E. *A Story, A Story.* Illustrated by Gail Haley. Atheneum, 1970.

McDermott, Gerald. *Anansi the Spider.* Illustrated by Gerald McDermott. Holt, 1972.

Sherlock, Philip. *Anansi the Spider Man: Jamaican Folk Tales.* Illustrated by Marcia Brown, Crowell, 1954.

2. In Bryan's "Ananse the Spider in Search of a Fool" in *The Ox of the Wonderful Horns*, Anansi is pictured as a spider. In *The Dancing Granny* Anansi is a dandy gentleman. Have students use the tales cited above to compare and contrast the manner in which illustrators have represented the character Anansi. Discuss how Anansi is given spiderlike qualities even when he is portrayed as a man.

3. Have students compare similar elements and story motifs (patterns) in *The Adventures of Aku* and "Jack and the Beanstalk."

4. Create a character web for Anansi/Ananse (see appendix A).

Bryan, Ashley, selector. **All Night, All Day.** Illustrated by Ashley Bryan. McElderry, 1991.

A collection of spirituals illustrated with block prints, this volume is a companion volume to *I'm Going to Sing: Black American Spirituals, Vol. II*, selected and illustrated by Ashley Bryan (Atheneum, 1982) and *Walk Together Children: Black American Spirituals*, selected and illustrated by Ashley Bryan (Atheneum, 1974). Each volume includes spirituals that celebrate the hopes and spirit of people who are trapped in slavery but bound together by their common heritage. (See notes on the history of spirituals that follow.)

1. Sing selected songs, varying them with each singing by improvising on the lyrics.

2. Find other folk songs that reflect cultural values. Compare the vitality of Bryan's renditions with others such as Robert Quackenbush's renditions of early American folk songs: *Clementine* (1974), *Go Tell Aunt Rhody* (1973), *The Man on the Flying Trapeze* (1972), *Old MacDonald Had a Farm* (1972), *Pop! Goes the Weasel and Yankee Doodle* (1976), *She'll Be Comin' Round the Mountain* (1973), and *Skip to My Lou* (1975) — all published by Lippincott.

3. Choose a favorite spiritual from one of Bryan's volumes to illustrate with your own images. Use watercolor or soft drawing pencils.

4. The illustrations for Bryan's books of spirituals are made with linoleum blocks. Make a linoleum block and use it to print an original logo for notecards. Directions for making linoleum prints may be found in art technique books. The school's art teacher may be able to recommend other techniques that will yield a similar result.

Notes on the History of Spirituals

Bryan's goal is to set down a total of 100 spirituals; the first volume of spirituals, *Walk Together Children: Black American Spirituals*, was just the beginning. Africans brought to America in chains created the first spirituals. From their African homeland, they brought with them their intricate African rhythms. As their sorrow of servitude threatened to crush them, they adopted the Christianity of their American masters. And so it was that they combined their age-old rhythms with biblical stories of hope and freedom. They choose their stories mainly from the Hebrew testament and turned them into melodious and spiritual musical offerings. The folk music became the brave cries of men and women forced to believe in a heaven because they had such little hope on earth.

In the first years after the Civil War, the newly emancipated African Americans wanted nothing that would remind them of their slavery. They cast off their moving melodies along with the chains that had bound them. The songs were little known outside of the South. Shortly after the Civil War, northern collectors set down the words and music, and in 1871 in a public performance, the Jubilee Singers of Fisk University in Nashville, Tennessee, brought the songs to the attention of a wider audience. Eventually the spirituals became famous throughout the world.

Over the years, new generations of African Americans learned the songs from their elders and sang them in church. Others began to pick up the songs as well. Bryan's goal is to provide a record of these songs and to preserve them for the young to learn and to sing.

Bryan, Ashley. **Beat the Story Drum, Pum-Pum.** Illustrated by Ashley Bryan. Atheneum, 1980.

The illustrations for these five tales were created with mostly black-and-white tempera paints. Red, black, and ochre paintings are interspersed throughout. *Beat the Story Drum, Pum-Pum* includes five Nigerian folk tales that represent universal motifs. Bryan's retellings are strong and rhythmic. Within each story text are appropriate actions, rhythms, and chants—and even changing voices (including animal noises) for each character. The stories share a common setting (Nigeria) and format but carry their own style and beat. They are filled with poetic devices: repetition, rhyming phrases, and alliteration. Source notes are included.

1. One of the stories included in this collection is "How the Animals Got Their Tails." It tells of the time when all animals were vegetarians. Then the creator, Raluvhimba, created a mistake. He created flies who were flesh-eaters and blood-suckers. He was unable to take back what he had done but did give the animals tails with which to swish away the flies. Read and discuss other pourquoi stories.

Pourquoi Stories

Aardema, Verna. *Why Mosquitoes Buzz in People's Ears: A West African Tale.* Illustrated by Leo Dillon and Diane Dillon. Dial, 1975.

Bryan, Ashley. *The Cat's Purr.* Illustrated by Ashley Bryan. Atheneum, 1985.

Carew, Jan. *The Third Gift.* Illustrated by Leo Dillon and Diane Dillon. Little, Brown, 1974.

Cole, Judith. *The Moon, the Sun, and the Coyote.* Illustrated by Cecile Schoberle. Simon, 1991.

Dayrell, Elphinstone. *Why the Sun and the Moon Live in the Sky.* Illustrated by Blair Lent. Houghton, 1968; reissued 1991.

Haley, Gail E. *A Story, A Story.* Illustrated by Gail E. Haley. Atheneum, 1970.

Kipling, Rudyard. *The Elephant's Child.* Illustrated by Edward Frascino. Simon, 1986.

Lester, Julius. *How Many Spots Does a Leopard Have? And Other Tales.* Illustrated by David Shannon. Scholastic, 1989.

Robbins, Ruth. *How the First Rainbow Was Made.* Illustrated by Ruth Robbins. Parnassus/Houghton, 1980.

2. These four stories are from folktales previously collected from the folklore of the Masai, the Bushmen, the Hausa, and peoples of Angola. Have students collect other information about these groups. For instance, the Masai live in East Africa, the Bushmen live in southern Africa, and the Hausa people live in northern Nigeria. How are these groups similar and how are they different?

3. Read additional tales from Nigeria retold in Harold Courlander's *The King's Drum and Other African Tales* (Harcourt, 1962). Chart the story grammar for each tale on a story map and compare and contrast the plots (see appendix A).

Bryan, Ashley. **The Cat's Purr.** Illustrated by Ashley Bryan. Atheneum, 1985.

A pourquoi West Indian story, *The Cat's Purr* tells of a rat stealing the cat's drum and explains "why cat eats rat." The rich language emulates the sounds of the animals' voices. Repeated throughout the story is the admonition "Remember now, don't rap it or beat it or tap it or poke it. Just stroke it gently. And don't let anyone else play it."

1. Tell or read the story, encouraging listeners to participate by repeating the refrain, "Remember now, ..." at the appropriate points in the story. Project the refrain on a screen, or write it on the chalkboard.

2. Build a thematic bridge between Bryan's *The Cat's Purr* and the poem "What the Gray Cat Sings" by Arthur Guiterman. Use Guiterman's poem for a choral reading, with alternate groups or solo voices reciting the verses. The entire group should join in the cat's weaving song—"Pr-rrum, pr-rrum, thr-ree, thr-reads, in the thr-rum, pr-rrum!"

3. Read and discuss other stories and poems featuring onomatopoetic text.

Books/Poems with Onomatopoetic Text

Aardema, Verna. *Why Mosquitoes Buzz in People's Ears: A West African Tale.* Illustrated by Leo Dillon and Diane Dillon. Dial, 1975.

cummings, e. e. *hist whist.* Illustrated by Deborah Kogan Ray. Crown, 1989. (poem)

Hutchins, Pat. *Good-Night, Owl!* Illustrated by Pat Hutchins. Macmillan, 1972.

McCord, David. "This Pickety Fence." In *Far and Few; Rhymes of Never Was and Always Is.* Illustrated by Henry B. Kane. Little, Brown, 1952. (poem)

Bryan, Ashley, illustrator. **Climbing Jacob's Ladder: Spirituals from the Old Testament.** Selected by John Langstaff. McElderry, 1991.

This is a companion volume to Bryan's *What a Morning! The Christmas Story in Black Spirituals.* For activity ideas see entry for that title.

Bryan, Ashley. **The Dancing Granny.** Illustrated by Ashley Bryan. Atheneum, 1977.

The Dancing Granny is a rhythmical tale from the Antilles. Granny Anika can't resist the song of the Spider Ananse (pictured as a vigorous young man). Spider Ananse tricks Granny Anika four times, but the old lady finally makes him dance with her.

1. Anansi tales, originally from Africa, took root in the western hemisphere when African slaves were brought to the Caribbean and the United States. In Jamaica Anansi became known as Brér Anansi, and in the southern United States the character was at times known as Aunt Nancy. Other southern tales feature a character similar to Anansi. Jack is a character who succeeds only through his wit and ingenuity. Many of the Jack tales have been collected by Richard Chase in *The Jack Tales* (Houghton, 1943). Compare Anansi to Jack as he is characterized in *The Jack Tales.* Help students use a character web to visualize each character's traits (see appendix A).

2. Many African tales are about personified animals, including the trickster spider Anansi. Other tricksters in African tales include Zomo, the rabbit, and Ijapa, the tortoise. Anansi and Zomo are both lazy characters who continually trick other animals into doing their work for them. Zomo became Brér Rabbit in the Black folklore of the United States when the Hausa people of Africa were brought to the western hemisphere as slaves.

   a. Read "Zomo Pays His Debts," in *Zomo the Rabbit* by Hugh Sturton, illustrated by Peter Warner (Atheneum, 1966).

   b. Compare Zomo to the Anansi character and to Brer Rabbit. Use the character web form (see appendix A), or create your own comparison chart on a large piece of tag board or the chalkboard.

   c. Use the catalog in your school or public library to locate collections of Brer Rabbit tales to read and compare with the Anansi tales you have found and read. Refer to the index of this book for other references to Brer Rabbit.

Bryan, Ashley, selector. **I'm Going to Sing: Black American Spirituals, Vol. II.** Illustrated by Ashley Bryan. Atheneum, 1982.

This volume of spirituals includes "Steal Away," "When the Saints," "Every Time I Feel the Spirit," "Rise Up Shepherd and Follow," "You Got a Right," and "Weary Traveler." Included are words and music that help children understand the importance of the spiritual and that promote the understanding of the importance of the spiritual to American heritage. The title page of this volume features a cherub with a trumpet, a common image found on the Gothic cathedrals of Europe. Activities suggested for the *All Night, All Day* entry will in most cases be equally appropriate for this title.

Bryan, Ashley, reteller. **Lion and the Ostrich Chicks and Other African Folk Tales.** Illustrated by Ashley Bryan. Atheneum, 1986.

Bryan's flowing woodcut illustrations in four colors and black and white aptly depict scenes for each of the four tales—each originating in a different African tribe.

1. "Lion and the Ostrich Chicks" is a Masai tale that tells of ostrich chicks that, showing the dim intelligence of their American cousin, the turkey, blunder into the lion's den and stay there.

   a. Read another Masai tale, Verna Aardema's *Who's in Rabbit's House?* (Dial, 1978). Compare the two stories. Do they have a common setting and a common origin? Explain.

   b. In Margaret Musgrove's *Ashanti to Zulu: African Traditions* (Dial, 1976) Musgrove presents a brief informational text for twenty-six African tribes. One of those tribes is the Masai. Leo Dillon and Diane Dillon's illustration for each section presents additional information about each tribe. Study the page featuring the Masai. On a large chart list all the information about the Masai that can be gleaned from the page. Then discuss how Bryan and Aardema incorporated facts about the Masai into their respective tales. A 17-minute filmstrip/cassette of Musgrove's *Ashanti to Zulu: African Traditions* is available from Weston Woods ® . This filmstrip will enable the Masai section to be projected, thus providing a larger image for the group to see.

2. Use a similar approach with the other stories in this collection.

Bryan, Ashley, reteller. **The Ox of the Wonderful Horns and Other African Folktales.** Illustrated by Ashley Bryan. Atheneum, 1971.

This collection of five tales from Africa is enriched with black-and-white tempera paintings highlighted with other images in red, black, and ochre. The longer tale uses the familiar motif of an outcast youth who gains love and success through the aid of magic. The shorter stories are about animals and their trickery.

1. One of the tales, "Ananse the Spider in Search of a Fool," is another of the Ananse/Anansi tales from Africa. In this tale it is Ananse that ends up doing all the work, thanks to the craftiness of Anene the Crow. Compare and contrast to other Ananse/Anansi stories. Correlate with responses for *The Adventures of Aku*.

2. Read other African tales, including Verna Aardema's *Oh, Kojo! How Could You?* (Dial, 1984) and tales in collections such as Aardema's *Behind the Back of the Mountain: Black Folktales from Southern Africa* (Dial, 1973). Find other African folktales by using the subject heading FOLKTALES—AFRICA.

Bryan, Ashley, reteller. **Sh-Ko and His Eight Wicked Brothers.** Illustrated by Fumio Yoshimura. Atheneum, 1988.

Sh-Ko and His Eight Wicked Brothers is illustrated in two colors by Bryan's friend Fumio Yoshimura. The story focuses on two ancient motifs: (1) the despised child (or stepchild) who triumphs over his or her evil siblings and (2) the kindhearted hero who is supernaturally aided by a grateful animal. Yoshimura uses animated brush drawings on buff-colored paper reminiscent of a twelfth-century masterpiece of Japanese caricature, the classic Scroll of Animals by Toba Sojo.

1. This tale has a motif of evil versus good. One character is obviously greedy and uncaring for others, while another character shares whatever he has and is kind and good to others. The motif is evidenced in many other folktales. Read the stories from the following list and compare the motifs.

Good vs. Evil Motif

Lattimore, Deborah Nourse. *The Dragon's Robe.* Illustrated by Deborah Nourse Lattimore. Harper, 1990.

San Souci, Robert D. *The Talking Eggs: A Folktale from the American South.* Illustrated by Jerry Pinkney. Dial, 1989.

Steptoe, John. *Mufaro's Beautiful Daughters: An African Tale.* Illustrated by John Steptoe. Lothrop, 1987.

Bryan, Ashley, reteller. **Turtle Knows Your Name.** Illustrated by Ashley Bryan. Atheneum, 1989.

In this story, which focuses on a young boy with a long name, the verbal images are as important as the visual ones. Repetition, rhythm, and rhyme are important elements in the narrative. A little boy is taught to walk and talk by his granny. When she teaches him his name, it takes time, because his name is Upsilimana

Tumpalerado. But Granny says, "Turtle takes his time, I take mine, and you take your time, too." When he finally learns his name, they go down to the sandy beach where they dance his "name dance" and sing his name into the sea. The turtle in the sea listens and remembers, but the boy's playmates cannot remember the long name. When the boy revisits the turtle, the turtle not only remembers the boy's name but also knows a secret name—the longest one of all. The watercolor paintings bring vitality and energy to the retelling. The story is retold from a collection of folklore from the Antilles.

1. Help students compare and contrast the dilemma in *Turtle Knows Your Name* to the problem in the Chinese pourquoi tale *Tikki Tikki Tembo* retold by Arlene Mosel (Holt, 1968).

2. *Tikki-Tikki-Tembo* is available in filmstrip, cassette, iconographic video, or 16-mm film format from Weston Woods ®. Use one of these formats for comparison and enjoyment of the Mosel tale.

3. Have students explain in their own words the significance of the secret name Turtle knows. Encourage students to share any secret names they have or know.

Bryan, Ashley. **Walk Together Children: Black American Spirituals.** Illustrated by Ashley Bryan. Atheneum, 1974; Aladdin, 1974.

This volume of more than twenty African-American spirituals includes "Little David," "Go Tell It on the Mountain," "Let Us Break Bread Together," "O What a Beautiful City," and "Rocking Jerusalem." The spirituals are religious songs, and Bryan strives to make a connection between the early block-printed religious books and his volume of spirituals. The elliptical shape of the block print that illustrates "In His Hands" is another reference to European religious heritage, thus establishing a connection between historical religious motifs and the music of African-Americans. Block cuts are used to illustrate the spirituals and to print the treble clef for each song. The accompanying verse appears in clear, large type. For activity ideas refer to the entry for *All Night, All Day.*

Bryan, Ashley, illustrator. **What a Morning! The Christmas Story in Black Spirituals.** Compiled by John Langstaff. Musical arrangements by John Andrew Ross. McElderry, 1987.

Bible verses and five black spirituals joyously celebrate the Christmas story in this chronological introduction to the Nativity. Guitar chords are provided as an alternative to the voice and piano arrangements. Bryan's rich, full-color, expressionistic paintings, created with tempera, are interspersed in the text of the spirituals to tell the story of the Nativity. The illustrations feature African motifs and a Black Holy Family. The "Note to Teachers, Parents and Instrumentalists" at the back of the book provides additional suggestions for using the book. For response ideas see the entry for *All Night, All Day.*

FURTHER READING

Another African-American illustrator who retells stories rooted in the African culture is Leo Dillon.[1] As an illustrator of books, Leo Dillon, with his wife Diane Dillon (who is not African American), has been awarded the Caldecott Medal twice. They received it the first time, in 1976, for Verna Aardema's *Why Mosquitoes Buzz in People's Ears* (Dial, 1975) and the following year for Margaret Musgrove's *Ashanti to Zulu* (Dial, 1976). Extend the focus on literature rooted in the African tradition by introducing students to books illustrated by the Dillons. Use the catalog in your school or public library to locate those books.

---

[1] Leo Dillon and Diane Dillon are featured in a section of *Bookpeople: A First Album* by Sharron L. McElmeel (Libraries Unlimited, 1990).

Ann Cameron

Ann Cameron

From *Bookpeople: A Multicultural Album* by Sharron L. McElmeel (Libraries Unlimited, Inc., 1992)

Ann Cameron

Ann Cameron was born October 21, 1943, in Rice Lake, Wisconsin. That is where she watched newborn pigs being warmed by a kitchen stove and where she heard stories of trolls and gremlins from her Swedish grandfather. When she grew up, she studied writing in college and worked in New York, California, Mexico, and Belize. One of her most interesting jobs was as camp cook, editor, and shard washer on a Mayan dig in the Yucatan jungle. She slept on a hammock in a thatched hut and lived surrounded by coral snakes, boa constrictors, and pit vipers.

Once she visited a friend in Guatemala and found the country so beautiful and interesting she decided to stay. So now she has an apartment in New York and a little house in Guatemala next door to a neighbor who, each morning, walks his three cows and a calf through his kitchen to get them to the pasture. Her own house has a garden, a lemon tree, a stone frog sitting in a fountain, and a view of three volcanoes.

Ann Cameron's South African friend Julian told her stories about his childhood. Those stories were the beginning of *The Stories Julian Tells*. She writes her stories on a computer in a one-room writing studio her husband, Bill Cherry, built for her. Recently she learned how to make homemade Italian pasta. She tosses sheets of pasta up in the air and bounces them around on her hands before cutting pasta shapes from the sheets. She also enjoys reading, gardening, cooking, swimming, and biking.

Ann Cameron

ABOUT THE AUTHOR

Rice Lake, Wisconsin, a small town of about 7,000 people, is Ann Cameron's hometown. She was born there on October 21, 1943, the daughter of William Cameron, a lawyer, and Lolita Cameron, a teacher. She has one sister, who is 7 years older. As Ann grew up she was filled with curiosity about other people. She read books by Louisa May Alcott, Mark Twain, Charles Dickens, and Laura Ingalls Wilder; the Mary Poppins books were also favorites. Her heroes included her dad, her uncle, a mythological character (Perseus), Robin Hood, Sacajawea, and the Lone Ranger. She attended Harvard, studied poetry with Robert Lowell, and graduated with honors in 1965. After Harvard, Cameron went to New York and worked in publishing. She edited and wrote evaluations of books at Harcourt Brace Jovanovich. In a personal interview in 1991, she recounted that her boss told her, "When you write your reports, tell me if a book is interesting and why."

That comment has stayed with Cameron, who says, "I think [that] is the most important question in reading and writing—knowing what interests you, and why." After 2 years as an editor, she knew that she wanted to be an author, not an editor. She was awarded a scholarship to the University of Iowa Writers Workshop and after 4 years of study, in 1972, was granted a master of fine arts degree from the university. She describes the next few years in her life as follows: "At that point I felt all I knew about was school and all I could do was read books and repeat what other people thought. So I left Iowa. I worked for a scientific company in Berkeley, California, and with archaeologists in Mexico and in Belize. I worked some more in publishing in New York and taught creative writing at Queens College; and I started figuring out what I thought and getting stories written, rather than analyzing what other people had thought. Of course, my own writing benefitted enormously from my reading, and my thoughts would not be much if I didn't know the literary tradition I'm part of."

She began writing poems and tried two adult novels. But the novels were "too big ... I hadn't much idea where I was going or when, if ever, I would finish." She then turned to writing for children; at least, she reasoned, she would get done. As a child, Cameron had had a friend, Bradley, who had a little sister. The three of them spent a lot of time together. Her childhood experiences became blended with those of a South African friend, Julian DeWette, who, as an adult, told her stories from his childhood. He spoke of a special friend he had named Gloria. His stories gave Cameron the initial inspiration for the Julian books. But the character Julian also has some similarity to Cameron when she was a child—for example, the two share a strong interest in nature and animals.

Cameron was once asked during a presentation why she wrote about races and cultures other than her own. Her response expressed disagreement with the basic premise that writers should write only about what they know. She feels that if all writers had followed that advice, Shakespeare would not have written of kings and queens, or about Italy or Egypt. Joseph Conrad would not have written about England, and Vladimir Nabokov would not have attempted to capture the spirit of the United States—after all, English was not his native language. Her advice to writers is, "Write about what you care about because what you care about, you *will* know." She does not think that there is such a thing as a literary territory that belongs to one group or another. Writers of any culture do not take the "field" away from someone else. If the book is successful, it is more than likely that someone else will find a publisher for an equally good or better book about that culture. "To think that a book lacks validity because someone of the 'wrong' nationality or ethnic group wrote it is only one more way of perpetuating racism in our country."[1] After the four books about

---

[1]Ann Cameron, "Write What You Care About," *School Library Journal* 35, no. 10 (June 1989): 51.

Julian were published, Cameron's editor thought it might be interesting if Cameron wrote a book about Gloria. At first she thought that was impossible, but later, after starting another project, she started getting ideas about Gloria and has begun to write a book about her.

Cameron's childhood interest in people has continued through the years. In New York she lives in a six-story walk-up apartment building just north of Greenwich Village, where she is surrounded by interesting people. Her neighbors include an organist and composer, a photographer, a sculptor, an artist who creates hand-painted textiles, a native of Peru (who is a public school guidance counselor), and a "big family of New Yorkers from Puerto Rico." On the bottom landing of the building's stairway is a window ledge. The ledge serves as a trading post for anyone who wishes to trade or give things away. At any one time the ledge might hold plants, books, magazines, or clothes. Cameron says, "I like things like this trading place; good customs that start up, nobody knows who begins them, but everyone carries them on."

In 1983, when Cameron traveled to Guatemala to visit a Guatemalan friend she had known in New York, she found the country so beautiful and interesting she decided to stay. She now has a little house in Panajachel, Guatemala, with a garden, a lemon tree, and a fountain that has water dripping out of the mouth of a stone frog. From her window she has a view of three enormous volcanoes. Her neighbor on one side is a Cachiquel Mayan Indian. Cameron says, "He keeps three cows and a calf in back of his house and walks them out through the kitchen of his house every morning to take them to pasture.... When I get up in the morning I water the garden, watch the cows, and walk to market to buy food — every kind of vegetable and fruit ... [you buy] from the person who picked it fresh the same morning, and you always bargain over the price. There is so much that's interesting here, I can't begin to describe it. One thing, though, is that very often on people's birthdays friends come at 5:00 in the morning and set off firecrackers outside your door to celebrate. And if they can afford it, they bring a marimba band to play for you and to sing."

In her acceptance speech for the 1989 Children's Book Award of the Child Study Children's Book Committee, Ann Cameron described how, because she has paper and crayons around, the neighborhood children come by her house to draw. One of those children is José Efrain. He became the model for *The Most Beautiful Place in the World*. Cameron says she and José are good friends and "Maybe I, the different person, the gringa, have become to him what the different people of my childhood were to me."[2]

In November 1990, Ann Cameron married Bill Cherry, recently retired from working for the United States Congress for the House Committee on Agriculture. When they married, Cameron suddenly had a new family. Cherry had two grown daughters, Angela and Cristi, and a 7-year-old granddaughter, Jessica. Cameron also acquired a mother-in-law, who "is 90 and keeps her own house and garden and cooks and waits on everybody who visits her." Cameron used to write all of her books in restaurants where owners would let her sit around for hours in the afternoon. Now she has a computer, which she is afraid will get stolen in the restaurants, so she works at home. Cherry built her a small one-room writing studio, with a fireplace, so she has a place to work.

Cameron spends much of her time in Panajachel. When she is not writing she enjoys reading, gardening, cooking, swimming, and biking. One of her newest interests is making homemade Italian pasta; she starts with flour and eggs and then rolls it out with a 3-foot-long rolling pin. "At first it was hard," she says, "but now I am so daring that I can throw the sheets of pasta up in the air and bounce them around on my hands to stretch them out." Her favorite foods are pasta, ice cream, hot chocolate, and homemade bread and pizza. She enjoys cats that will allow you to rub your nose against their stomachs. She has two cats, Jane and Special. Her life seems guided by her belief that, "when I do what really matters to me, I'm happy, and my friends are real friends who like me for what I really am."

---

[2]Ibid.

THE BOOKSHELF

Cameron, Ann. **Julian, Secret Agent.** Illustrated by Diane Worfolk Allison. Random, 1988. (Stepping Stone Books)

Julian, his little brother Huey, and his best friend, Gloria, decide to be crimebusters after seeing the most-wanted posters in the post office. But their discoveries lead to some funny times. They do manage to help save a dog from heat exhaustion and someone from drowning. But the "most-wanted" person turns out to be the police chief's son.

1. Extend the interest in solving mysteries by having students read any of the Encyclopedia Brown mystery books by Donald Sobol or the Cam Jansen detective books by David A. Adler. Discuss what makes a mystery exciting.

2. Have students make a wanted poster for Eugene George Johnson. What do students think Eugene looks like and what was his crime? What had he done in Topeka?

Cameron, Ann. **Julian's Glorious Summer.** Illustrated by Dora Leder. Random, 1987. (Stepping Stone Books)

When Gloria gets a new bike, Julian, a seven-year-old Black child, is upset; he doesn't want to learn to ride because he is afraid he will fall. But in the end Julian gets his own bike and learns what fun it is to ride.

1. Share and read other books that deal with bikes and bike riding.

Bikes and Biking

Delton, Judy. *A Birthday Bike for Brimhall.* Illustrated by June Leary. Carolrhoda, 1985.

Lindgren, Astrid. *Lotta's Bike.* Illustrated by Ilon Wikland. Farrar, 1990.

Strub, Susanne. *Lulu on Her Bike.* Illustrated by Susanne Strub. Viking, 1990.

2. Give students large sheets of butcher paper on which to make full-sized drawings of a bicycle. Have them work with a partner. If several bicycles are drawn, display them as if they are in a bicycle tour or race.

3. Ask students to write about the first time they rode a bike.

4. Students should be encouraged to explore their own fears with these questions. Were you ever scared to do something? Tell about it or draw a picture showing you when you finally got up the courage to do it. If you've never been afraid of trying something, what would make you scared?

Cameron, Ann. **More Stories Julian Tells.** Illustrated by Ann Strugnell. Knopf, 1986.

Julian, his friend Gloria, and his younger brother Huey are back in five stories. The incidents include: (1) making a bet with a friend (sometimes frogs do wear shoes); (2) sending a message in a bottle (does the river near Julian's house flow straight to the sea?); (3) attempting to be brave (as brave as Superboy); (4) name calling; and (5) moving the sun (Gloria can *with help*).

1. Have students tell about something unusual they have done with a friend.

2. Read the following books about good friends.

Friendships

Aliki. *The Two of Them.* Illustrated by Aliki. Greenwillow, 1979.

Brown, Marc. *The True Francine.* Illustrated by Marc Brown. Little, Brown, 1981.

Carle, Eric. *Do You Want to Be My Friend?* Illustrated by Eric Carle. Crowell, 1971.

Ehrlich, Amy. *Leo, Zack, and Emmie.* Illustrated by Steven Kellogg. Dial, 1981.

Giff, Patricia Reilly. *I Love Saturday.* Illustrated by Frank Remkiewicz. Viking, 1989.

Hest, Amy. *The Best-Ever Good-Bye Party.* Illustrated by DyAnne DiSalvo-Ryan. Morrow, 1989.

Hoban, Lillian. *Best Friends for Francis.* Illustrated by Lillian Hoban. Harper, 1969.

Hutchins, Pat. *What Game Shall We Play?* Illustrated by Pat Hutchins. Greenwillow, 1990.

Lobel, Arnold. *Frog and Toad Are Friends.* Illustrated by Arnold Lobel. Harper, 1970. (There are several other books by Lobel about Frog and Toad.)

Marshall, James. *George and Martha.* Illustrated by James Marshall. Houghton, 1972. (There are several other books by Marshall about George and Martha.)

McPhail, David. *Lost!* Illustrated by David McPhail. Joy Street, 1990.

Oxenbury, Helen. *Tom and Pippo Make a Friend.* Illustrated by Helen Oxenbury. Aladdin, 1989. (Four books are in the Pippo series.)

Velthuijs, Max. *Elephant and Crocodile.* Illustrated by Max Velthuijs. Farrar, 1990.

Friends
(for read-alouds and intermediate readers)

Delton, Judy. *Kitty in the Middle.* Houghton, 1979.

Derby Pat. *Goodbye Emily, Hello.* Farrar, 1989.

Gaeddert, Lou Ann. *Your Former Friend, Matthew.* Dutton, 1984.

Hurwitz, Johanna. *The Hot and Cold Summer.* Morrow, 1978.

Marney, Dean. *Just Good Friends.* Addison, 1982.

Cameron, Ann. **The Most Beautiful Place in the World.** Illustrated by Thomas B. Allen. Knopf, 1988.

Juan, a Guatemalan boy, triumphs over abandonment and poverty. Both parents have left him, but he is cared for by his grandmother. He works as her helper in the marketplace. Later he is a shoeshine boy in front of the Tourist Office, where he teaches himself to read from scraps of newspaper. But Juan has dreams of learning more. He finds the courage to ask if he can go to school.

1. Locate Guatemala on a map.

2. Discuss with students how Juan's life is different from or the same as theirs.

3. Discuss the opportunities education offers. Ask students to list ten reasons why they like to go to school.

Cameron, Ann. **The Stories Julian Tells.** Illustrated by Ann Strugnell. Knopf, 1981.

Julian tells stories of his family and of childhood mischief. Julian and his family are Black. Julian and his brother Huey get into the lemon pudding, find real catalog cats, plant the family garden, have trouble because of a surprising, different birthday present, and deal with the oddity of having two teeth in one space. The final story discusses "Gloria who might be my best friend."

1. Make lemon pudding like the boys did in the story.

2. Eat a fig. Discuss the following with students: Would you want a fig tree for your birthday? Why or why not?

3. Write a story about the first tooth you remember losing. Was it pulled out with pliers or a string? Did you pull it?

4. Make a picture of you doing something special with your best friend.

FURTHER READING

Ann Cameron grew up in the Midwest, and her presence in this multicultural resource book is based on the subject matter of her books. Her tales of Julian, a Black child, are stories with which most young children will be able to identify. Do some wide reading in realistic fiction and picture books. Make a chart with a space for each book's main activity, a column for the main characters' ethnicity, a yes column, and a no column. As you read each story fill in the columns of the chart. The yes and no columns will indicate whether or not the majority of the class members would likely have had or might yet have a similar experience. Think in terms of generalities. For example, in one story Julian and his brother get into lemon pudding. It is likely that more children will recognize their own similar behavior if the activity is stated as "getting into something that they should not" than if it is stated as specifically getting into lemon pudding.

Donald Crews

Donald Crews

Ann Jonas and Donald Crews

TRUCKING

From *Bookpeople: A Multicultural Album* by Sharron L. McElmeel (Libraries Unlimited, Inc., 1992)

Donald Crews

Donald Crews spent his childhood in Newark, New Jersey, where he was born on August 30, 1938. A high school teacher encouraged him to make art his career and to attend New York City's Cooper Union School. He was in the army in Germany when he designed his first book, *We Read: A to Z*. It was published 5 or 6 years later in 1967.

While growing up Donald Crews took many trips to his grandparents' farm in Florida, where he saw many freight trains. Those memories gave him the idea to create *Freight Train*. Its popularity encouraged him to make more books. Ideas came from his view of the harbor, bicycle races in Central Park, and trucks at the depot by his home. He often includes bits of information about himself or his family in his illustrations: "N & A" on a steam engine are the first letters of his children's names, and boats in the harbor are named for family and friends.

Both Donald Crews and his artist wife, Ann Jonas, have art and design studios in their brownstone house in Brooklyn, New York. They have two grown daughters, Nina and Amy, a very big dog, and a small cat. Both artists are said to be good cooks, and German food is a particular favorite of Donald's.

Donald Crews

ABOUT THE AUTHOR/ILLUSTRATOR

Born on August 30, 1938, in Newark, New Jersey, Donald Crews grew up and attended public schools there. He had two sisters and one brother. He always enjoyed doing things with his hands and, like many other children, he liked to color with crayons. But he did not think about making a career of art until he attended Arts High School, a specialized school that required a competitive examination for admission. A teacher there recognized his talent and encouraged him to get more training in the arts. But his older brother was studying to be a medical doctor when it came time for Donald to go to college, and knowing his father's railroad salary would not stretch enough to allow him to go to college, too, Donald was ready to set his own training aside. But the teacher encouraged him to attend the tuition-free Cooper Union School for the Advancement of Science and Arts in New York City. It was there that he met his future wife, Ann Jonas. After completing college and working for 2 years, Crews served in the military in Germany, where he was a military policeman. Ann Jonas came to Germany to be with him, and they were married and had their first daughter, Nina, there. That is also where he assigned himself the task of designing his first picture book, *We Read: A to Z*. He created the book in an 8-inch by 8-inch format, since that was just the right size to work on at the small table they had in their home. The book was intended to become part of his design portfolio, but an editor at Harper & Row liked it well enough to publish it in 1967. By this time their second daughter, Amy, had been born. Crews then created *Ten Black Dots*, a companion volume to his earlier alphabet book. When Scribner published it in 1968, he received many requests to illustrate books by other writers. Crews has said that creating picture books gives him a chance to show his ability to design, and to show his mother that he does things. For 10 years he illustrated books by other writers and accepted other art projects. These included designing a book jacket for *Jazz Country* by Nat Hentoff (Harper, 1965) and one for a book of ethnic poetry edited by David Kheridan. He illustrated two books by Harry Milgrom: *ABC Science Experiments* (Macmillan, 1973) and *ABC of Ecology* (Macmillan, 1976). In the ecology title he used a photograph of his older daughter, Nina, on the "I" page (she had an "idea").

After several years he decided to try creating another book of his own. He was not pleased with the texts of some of the books he was being asked to illustrate and decided that instead of complaining about it he would write one of his own. The fact that he would get to keep all the royalties did not escape him. He set out to find a topic for his book. As a young child he had often traveled to Florida with his parents to see his grandparents. On the way there, they saw many freight trains pulled by steam locomotives. And once they arrived, Donald would spend hours every day counting the trains as they passed by the porch of the big house in Cottondale. Those images came back to him as he planned his book. He knew he wanted to introduce a spectrum of color as well as simple shapes. His memories, combined with his design skill, resulted in *Freight Train*. The book is a riot of color as the train whizzes past the reader's eyes. Various types of train cars chug along the track until they build up enough speed to make the train a magnificent blur of speed and color across a double-page spread. Crews builds anticipation by using five white background pages of track as the reader waits for the train to pass. A concise and accurate description of each freight car follows on the next eight pages. Each freight car is correctly named according to its function. The cars are colored vivid red, orange, yellow, green, blue, and purple and are accented by black verticals, horizontals, circles, and squares. The grayish clouds of smoke and tunnels of black and gray bring needed contrast. The technique Crews employs most often is vivid color outlined in black. His artwork, most of which is characterized by bright colors, graphic lettering, city signs, and diagonal lines, shows the influence of pop artists, especially Robert Indiana. Crews's books are often cited as having begun a trend toward the simple and realistic and toward easily identifiable characters.

Crews took *Freight Train* to an editor at Greenwillow, Susan Hirschman, who wanted to buy the book after seeing just two or three pages. Her instincts were good, as *Freight Train* was named a Caldecott honor book in 1979. The book's success made Crews enough money to convince him that he might be able to make a living doing children's books.

His next book, *Truck*, was inspired by a scene he saw often. At the time, he lived in a loft on lower Broadway. In his neighborhood was a truck depot area where trucks were loaded and dispatched. He liked the idea of a book that investigated where the trucks went after they left the depot. The thumbnail sketches he began to make for *Truck* helped him plan the book. He especially wanted to emphasize the size of the trucks. He also wanted young readers to identify with the truck's journey, so he loaded a truck with tricycles. He used changing size to suggest movement as the trucks traveled from New York to California. To show the travel accurately he had to get pictures of the countryside in New York and Colorado and other places along the way. He took a lot of photographs so he could study what trucks did and where they went. Children who have traveled along an expressway will recognize many of the scenes. For those who have not traveled those byways, this book provides an opportunity for them to leave their own neighborhoods and to develop conversational skills and a richer vocabulary.

For his book *Light*, Crews began his planning, as he usually does, with research pictures and thumbnail sketches of the idea. He tried to show the contrast between city and country. One of the city scenes shows the clock tower on the Cooper Union building, where he attended art school.

When the Crews family moved from Manhattan to Brooklyn, they crossed the Brooklyn Bridge, and the charm of the harbor and the river gave Crews the idea to create a book about rivers—from small mountain streams to full-blown river floods. Crews thought the idea was terrific, but his editors hated it. When he expanded the harbor pages, his editors liked it a little bit more. When he expanded the harbor pages again, they bought the book but then decided they really didn't like it. Finally Crews took just the harbor scenes and expanded them into a book his editors liked and published, *Harbor*. The scene of the harbor wharf is from the perspective of a viewer looking toward Brooklyn Heights.

The story in *Bicycle Race* is simple. Crews's illustrations help us to focus our eyes on number 9; and we are, of course, encouraged to cheer for number 9 as the cyclist weaves in and out in the tight race. Our cheers led him on to win—as we knew they would.

For the book *Parade*, Crews researched a football band and nine soldiers standing in rank. He had not done human figures up to this time, so he decided to render the people abstractly and to concentrate his detailed artwork on the background for the parade. The parade units move from the back forward. The idea for another book, *Carousel*, came from a real carousel at Coney Island. He took many photographs of the carousel before he began. Once he had done the collage illustrations, he moved the camera lens across the finished art so that the resulting photographs would give the effect of a whirling carousel. Crews's earlier books were printed from color-separated art, but his later ones, including *Carousel*, are printed from his full-color artwork.

Crews often puts bits and pieces of other books or snippets of his family in a current book. In his book *Flying*, he places himself in the lower left-hand corner of the boarding picture. In *Flying*, close observers can spot a tugboat and a truck or two from some of his other books. In *Bicycle Race* Crews puts his arm around his wife, and in *School Bus*, he shows himself, carrying his portfolio, crossing the street. In *Freight Train*, the black steam engine carries the name of the railroad, N & A — the initials of his two daughters, Nina and Amy. The black coal car bears, in large orange numerals, the date the book was published. In *Truck*, published in 1980, the numeral 79 appears on a van in a long line of vehicles traveling through the countryside. That would indicate that the artwork was completed in 1979. The numeral 81 appears on a pier in *Harbor*, and 1982 is conveniently split between the street sweepers cleaning up before and after the festivities in *Parade*.

Crews also has fun with his dedications. His first book, *We Read: A to Z*, is dedicated quite simply and reads, "Particularly for Ann, Nina, Amy, Donna, Janine, Michael, and Zönke." And his dedication for *Freight Train* is not necessarily as poetic as it is informative. It reads, "With due respect to Casey Jones, John Henry, the Rock Island Line, and the countless freight trains passed and passing the big house in Cottondale." But the dedication for *Flying* is "For those who make my heart soar." And in *Carousel* the dedication is also a visual exercise, reading, "For 'MAMANNINAMY' spinning together." Here we see, all strung together, Mama, Ann, Nina, Amy. In *Light* the dedication includes a list of names concluded by "Bright Lights one and all."

Ann Jonas, Crews's wife, is also a designer and artist who has created some picture books of her own. Both artists have a studio in their brownstone house in Brooklyn. The garden floor is rented out, and the Crewses live in the top three floors. The back of their second floor holds Jonas's studio. Upstairs, on the very top floor, are two bedrooms and Crews's studio. He spends time each day in his studio, where he does all of his sketching and art work, but he also likes to walk around in the streets during "working hours." He says he's not really playing hooky, he's doing research. The Crewses have a garden in their backyard, and both enjoy cooking on their six-burner commercial gas range. At various times they have shared their home with a very large dog and a very tiny kitten. The two Crews daughters, Nina and Amy, are in their late twenties. Both attended Yale University, where Nina studied art and Amy majored in journalism.

THE BOOKSHELF

Donald Crews's books are basically concept books that convey an idea through the illustrations. Most of the illustrations are collages incorporating bright colors, bold designs, sharp graphic lettering, and inventive ideas. In some of his later books Crews has utilized a moving camera lens to make photographs that suggest fast movement. Sometimes he uses airbrush painting to enhance the images.

Crews's books are usually classified as books for the preschooler or early primary child. That classification is appropriate if the books are considered primary reading material. However, the books could be used with much older groups to provide a starting point for a focus. For example, if a unit on school bus safety is part of the curriculum, one might want to start the unit with Crews's *School Bus*. *Truck* provides very young children an opportunity to read environmental print, but it can also begin a focus on shapes of highway signs for preteenagers who will need to know those shapes when they take their driving tests. Many of Crews's books can motivate or extend activities for readers of various ages. The age and experience of your students will influence the specific manner in which you use the following suggestions, which can be used with a focus from any of Crews's books.

Response Suggestions for Any of Crews's Books

1. Write a narration for the book, following the journey that is taken in the book.

2. Create a collage depicting trucks, boats, planes, or whatever topic is shown in the book. Cut pictures out of magazines or newspapers, or make original collages from cut paper shapes.

3. Donald Crews says that he tries to give information in his books. Look for information about the topic or setting as you look at each book. Make a list of information found in the book.

4. Search the book for information about Crews and his family.

5. Make a three-dimensional object to depict the book. For example, after reading *Truck*, create a truck from boxes and cardboard; after reading *Flying*, make paper or balsa wood airplanes.

6. Try using a stencil airbrush to create puffy clouds as seen in *Freight Train*, the spraying water as seen coming from the fire boat in *Harbor*, or the blur of the passing horses in *Carousel*.

7. After discussing the idea of a "metaphorical" dedication, use an example from one of Crews's books, and make a list of the other dedications from his other books. Then the next time a classmate "publishes" a book in the classroom, help the author write a creative dedication.

8. Organize an "I Love Donald Crews Week." Make posters depicting each of his books.

9. Display objects that represent Crews's books, involving students when appropriate.

10. Chart the route that your truck (or plane, or train) would take across the country.

11. Construct your own carousel.

12. Culminate your week with a read-in. Invite older readers to share a book with a group of younger readers. At the end of the final day, celebrate with peanuts (from your airplane flight) and a rousing 5 minutes of music (a march from the parade).

The following ideas are for the specific books listed.

Crews, Donald. **Bicycle Race.** Illustrated by Donald Crews. Greenwillow, 1985.

The words in this action-filled book help the readers follow the race. Because the positions of the racers change with every page, readers must watch the numbers on the racers' backs.

1. Use a cassette recorder to record a "radio broadcast" of the bicycle race. Share with another group.

2. Practice riding bikes for your own bicycle race.

3. Cut out pictures of bicycles and make your own bicycle race collage.

4. Create a bicycle race board game complete with directions.

Crews, Donald. **Bigmama's**. Illustrated by Donald Crews. Greenwillow, 1991.

Crews remembers as a child the summers spent on the porch of Bigmama's house in Florida. The entire family journeyed to visit their grandmother Bigmama. Cousins were reunited and spent so much time talking that they hardly had time to eat. Depicted in bold graphics, buildings are set against the lush foliage of the Florida countryside. The final two pages depict a jet black night sky with millions of shining stars, a sky that promised wonderful things at Bigmama's. Even now such a sky brings back memories of Bigmama's.

1. Compare the family unity that is the focus of this book with the family unity present in Cynthia Rylant's *The Relatives Came*, illustrated by Stephen Gammell (Bradbury, 1985). Discuss the activities and memories evoked by each book. Compare one of these reunions with your family reunion.

2. On a map locate the northern Florida town of Cottondale in the Panama City, Florida, area. Crews writes about the reunions at his grandmother's house during the 1930s. Find out about the town as it is today. The town does not have a chamber of commerce nor does it seem to have a public library. Encourage children to use their thinking skills to brainstorm a list of ways that they might locate information about the town. The town's zip code is 32431.

Crews, Donald. **Carousel.** Illustrated by Donald Crews. Greenwillow, 1982.

The carousel is still and empty and the calliope is silent. Then people step onto the platform and climb onto their mounts. The horses begin to go up and down and round and round. The horses begin to blur as they race into each other and become one blended hue. The carousel gradually begins to slow down, finally stops, and is still once again.

1. Draw or paint a carousel horse. Make it unique and interesting. If you are real adventurous, make a papier-mâché horse.

2. Make a three-dimensional carousel. If you can, make it turn and move round and round.

3. Look at the carousel Uncle Ezra made for Bizzy Bones in Jacqueline Briggs Martin's *Uncle Ezra and Bizzy Bones* (Lothrop, 1984). What other objects or animals might be put on a carousel? Make a list, draw a picture, and make a prototype of your own unique carousel.

Crews, Donald. **Flying.** Illustrated by Donald Crews. Greenwillow, 1986.

Board the plane and soar over highways and rivers, cities and mountains, across the countryside. *Flying* lets the reader experience the excitement of takeoff, changing scenery, and finally, landing.

1. Read Byron Barton's *Airport* (Crowell, 1982) and compare the perspectives each book presents.

2. Use Seymour Simon's *Paper Airplane Book* (Viking, 1971) to make paper airplanes. Fly them and measure the distance each one flies. After practicing, enter in a "fly-off" the five that are able to travel the longest distance. Chart the distances on the board.

3. Read about a real flight, *The Glorious Flight: Across the Channel with Louis Blériot, July 25, 1909*, by Alice and Martin Provensen (Viking, 1983). Or use Robert Burleigh's *Flight: The Journey of Charles Lindbergh* (Philomel, 1991). Then research other significant milestones in the history of flight. Make a time line. Tom Snyder Productions, Inc., has a computer program called Timeliner that can help students create the time line.

Crews, Donald. **Freight Train.** Illustrated by Donald Crews. Greenwillow, 1978.

From back to front, the cars of a freight train—a red caboose, an orange tank car, a yellow hopper car, a green cattle car, a blue gondola car, a purple box car, a black tender, and finally the black steam engine— are ready to roll down the tracks, through tunnels, by cities, and over trestles. Once the train is moving, it blurs into a flash of color—until it emerges from the darkness into the daylight and moves out of sight.

1. Emerging readers can soon read *Freight Train* and tape it onto a cassette recording for others to listen to in a listening center. Be sure to encourage sound effects (klickity-klack on the railroad tracks).

2. Provide tempera paint and large pieces of paper so that children can paint a favorite train car. Encourage them to mix and match colors and cars.

3. After children have painted their train cars as suggested in activity 2, display the cars labeled with their color and name, for example, "purple hopper car."

4. Extend students' interest in trains by reading *Trains* by Gail Gibbons (Holiday, 1987).

5. Share with students *Train Song*, a rhyming account of a train rolling through the countryside, written by Diane Siebert, illustrated by Mike Wimmer (Crowell, 1990).

6. Provide paper shaped like train cars and engines on which students can write train information and stories.

Crews Donald. **Harbor.** Illustrated by Donald Crews. Greenwillow, 1982.

Liners, tankers, tugs, barges, ferryboats, and lighters — all are part of the traffic that goes through the harbor — a harbor full of color, movement, and excitement.

1. Extend the theme of boats and boating by reading some of the following titles:

Boats and Boating

Demi, reteller. *The Magic Boat.* Illustrated by Demi. Holt, 1990.

Hest, Amy. *A Sort-of Sailor.* Illustrated by Lizzy Rockwell. Four Winds, 1990.

Pfanner, Louise. *Louise Builds a Boat.* Illustrated by Louise Pfanner. Orchard, 1990.

Stevenson, James. *The Stowaway.* Illustrated by James Stevenson. Greenwillow, 1990.

2. Create a class dictionary of boats. For each entry, draw a picture, tell something about the specific boat or ship pictured, and then arrange the entries alphabetically.

Crews, Donald. **Light.** Illustrated by Donald Crews. Greenwillow, 1981.

This book contrasts city and country, light and dark. Look for the clock tower at Cooper Union, the art school Crews attended.

1. Help students locate information about country living and the night environment in the country in the following titles.

In the Country

Rylant, Cynthia. *Night in the Country.* Illustrated by Mary Szilagyi. Bradbury, 1986.

Stolz, Mary. *Storm in the Night.* Illustrated by Pat Cummings. HarperCollins, 1988.

Yolen, Jane. *Owl Moon.* Illustrated by John Schoenherr. Philomel, 1987.

2.   Have students draw a picture of their neighborhood or house as it would look at night and another picture to show the same scene in the daytime. Discuss how such differences can be artistically portrayed.

Crews, Donald. **Parade.** Illustrated by Donald Crews. Greenwillow, 1983.

The parade watchers look toward the back, see the beginning of the parade, and watch as page after page of paraders march past the crowd.

1.   Create a class parade mural. Give students, working in pairs, a large piece of butcher paper. Ask them to draw their parade entry on the paper. Crayons or tempera paints may be used to fill in the color. Once the drawing is completed, the parade entry should be cut out and, along with all the other parade entries, glued onto a long strip of butcher paper to create the finished mural.

2.   March with students around the room to a marching tune.

Crews, Donald. **School Bus.** Illustrated by Donald Crews. Greenwillow, 1984.

The buses are shown in various places, but each one picks up children in the morning and delivers them back to their homes at the end of the day.

1.   Make a list of the signs that children should watch for when they are riding and walking. Discuss the colors, shapes, and functions of each sign.

2.   Make a dictionary of signs.

3.   Make a map of the route a school bus would take if it were picking you up at your front door, taking you to school, and then returning you home at the end of the day. Model the map-making exercise, then ask each student to create his or her own map.

Crews, Donald. **Ten Black Dots.** Illustrated by Donald Crews. Scribner's, 1968; rev. ed., Greenwillow, 1986.

This counting book of simple rhymes using everyday objects asks the question, "What can you do with ten black dots?"

1.   Think of new ideas for each set of dots 1-10. Draw the illustrations and bind your pages into a book.

2.   Read other counting books. Write another counting book. Use your own ideas. Some of the following counting books might give you some ideas.

Counting Books

Anno, Mitsumasa. *Anno's Counting Book.* Illustrated by Mitsumasa Anno. Crowell, 1977.

Archambault, John. *Counting Sheep.* Illustrated by John Rombola. Holt, 1989.

Aylesworth, Jim. *One Crow: A Counting Rhyme*. Illustrated by Ruth Young. Lippincott, 1988.

Backman, Aidel. *One Night, One Hanukkah Night*. Illustrated by Aidel Backman. Jewish, 1990.

Bang, Molly. *Ten, Nine, Eight*. Illustrated by Molly Bang. Greenwillow, 1983.

Chouinard, Roger, and Mariko Chouinard. *One Magic Box*. Doubleday, 1989.

Coats, Laura Jane. *Ten Little Animals*. Illustrated by Laura Jane Coats. Macmillan, 1990.

Crossley-Holland, Kevin. *Under the Sun and Over the Moon*. Putnam, 1989.

Dunbar, Joyce. *Ten Little Mice*. Illustrated by Maria Majewska. Harcourt, 1990.

Dunrea, Olivier. *Deep Down Underground*. Illustrated by Olivier Dunrea. Macmillan, 1989.

Ehlert, Lois. *Fish Eyes: A Book You Can Count On*. Illustrated by Lois Ehlert. Harcourt, 1990.

Hayes, Sarah. *Nine Ducks Nine*. Illustrated by Sarah Hayes. Lothrop, 1990.

MacCarthy, Patricia. *Ocean Parade: A Counting Book*. Illustrated by Patricia MacCarthy. Dial, 1990.

Morozumi, Atsuko. *One Gorilla: A Counting Book*. Farrar, 1990.

Oliver, Stephen. *My First Look at Numbers*. Illustrated by Stephen Oliver. Random, 1990.

Scott, Ann Herbert. *One Good Horse: A Cowpuncher's Counting Book*. Greenwillow, 1990.

Sheppard, Jeff. *The Right Number of Elephants*. Harper, 1990.

Thornhill, Jan. *The Wildlife 1-2-3: A Nature Counting Book*. Illustrated by Jan Thornhill. Simon, 1989.

Crews, Donald. **Truck.** Illustrated by Donald Crews. Greenwillow, 1980.

The large rear doors of a semitrailer truck shut on a load of tricycles ready for shipment. The red diesel truck slowly moves onto the busy city streets, maneuvers into position in the tunnel, and stops at an all-night truck stop for food and fuel. The driver shifts down to travel rain-soaked highways, cross endless level intersections, and crawl over foggy bridges. The truck finally reaches the delivery dock at its destination.

1. Much environmental print is inherent in this minimal-text book. Expand on the use of environmental print—road and street signs, store signs, etc.—by introducing students to some of the following books.

Environmental Print

Crews, Donald. *School Bus*. Illustrated by Donald Crews. Greenwillow, 1984.

Goor, Ron, and Nancy Goor. *Signs*. Crowell, 1983.

Hoban, Tana. *I Read Signs*. Illustrated by Tana Hoban. Greenwillow, 1983.

Hoban, Tana. *I Read Symbols.* Illustrated by Tana Hoban. Greenwillow, 1983.

Preston, Edna Mitchell. *Where Did My Mother Go?* Illustrated by Chris Conover. Four Winds, 1978.

2. Extend the theme of trucking by sharing *Truck Song* by Diane Siebert, illustrated by Byron Barton (Crowell, 1984). Siebert presents a ballad of a truck driver's cross-country haul.

3. Share another truck story. Try some of those on the following list.

Trucks and Trucking

Bushey, Jerry. *Monster Trucks: And Other Giant Machines on Wheels.* Carolrhoda, 1985.

Gibbons, Gail. *Trucks.* Illustrated by Gail Gibbons. Crowell, 1981.

Kessler, Ethel, and Leonard P. Kessler. *Night Story.* Illustrated by Leonard P. Kessler. Macmillan, 1981.

Rockwell, Anne. *Trucks.* Dutton, 1984.

4. Create a travel and mileage log for the driver of *Truck.*

Crews, Donald. **We Read: A to Z.** Illustrated by Donald Crews. Harper, 1967; Greenwillow, 1984.

Using all twenty-six letters, Crews illustrates, with words and graphics created in bright bold colors, concepts such as almost, bottom, jagged, and other terms not easily visualized. This is a most unusual alphabet book that needs more adult participation than just reading it aloud. The concepts will need to be discussed and played with.

1. Make your own graphic representation of the concept presented for each letter. For example, "Aa, almost: nearly, nearly all filled" could be illustrated with a nearly filled glass of water. Or "Ee, equal: as many red as white" might be illustrated with an equal number of alternating red and white stripes (as with the American flag). Try your illustrative hand on other concepts.

2. Read other alphabet books. Alphabet books can be located by using the subject heading ALPHABET BOOKS in your school or public library or by consulting booklists contained in reference books such as Carolyn W. Lima's *A to Zoo: Subject Access to Children's Picture Books* (Bowker, 1989) or Sharron McElmeel's *My Bag of Book Tricks* (Libraries Unlimited, 1989). The following is a starter list.

Alphabet Books

Bayer, Jane. *A My Name Is Alice.* Illustrated by Steven Kellogg. Dutton, 1984.

Cameron, Elizabeth. *A Wildflower Alphabet.* Morrow, 1984.

Ehlert, Lois. *Eating the Alphabet.* Harcourt, 1989.

Jonas, Ann. *Aardvarks, Disembark!* Illustrated by Ann Jonas. Greenwillow, 1990.

Lobel, Anita. *Alison's Zinnia.* Illustrated by Anita Lobel. Greenwillow, 1990.

Mayer, Marianna. *The Unicorn Alphabet*. Illustrated by Michael Hague. Dial, 1989.

Pallotta, Jerry. *The Frog Alphabet Book: And Other Awesome Amphibians*. Illustrated by Ralph Masiello. Charlesbridge, 1990. (Pallotta has several other animal/bird alphabet books. All are published by Charlesbridge.)

Sis, Peter. *Beach Ball*. Illustrated by Peter Sis. Greenwillow, 1990.

Wells, Carolyn. *A Christmas Alphabet*. Putnam, 1989.

FURTHER READING

Byron Barton has a similar graphic and minimal-word technique for creating books. Some of his titles are *Airport* (Crowell, 1982), *Bones, Bones, Dinosaur Bones* (Crowell, 1990), *I Want to Be an Astronaut* (Crowell, 1988), *Dinosaurs, Dinosaurs* (Crowell, 1989), and *Machines at Work* (Crowell, 1987). Read some of his books and compare his illustrative technique with Crews's.

Pat Cummings

From *Bookpeople: A Multicultural Album* by Sharron L. McElmeel (Libraries Unlimited, Inc., 1992)

Pat Cummings

Pat Cummings was born November 9, 1950. While she was growing up, she moved with her father, an army man, to Virginia, Kansas, and such faraway places as Germany and Okinawa. Her art helped her make new friends wherever she moved. When she was in the fifth grade, she sold drawings, especially those of ballerinas, to her classmates.

Now Pat Cummings lives in a loft overlooking the waterfront in Brooklyn, New York, where she draws and paints for a living. If she looks out the back window of her loft, she can see the Statue of Liberty, and from her rooftop she can see many of the same New York city scenes that Chuku sees in her book *C.L.O.U.D.S.* When she paints pictures for her books she often includes her husband and other relatives and friends. She shows her work area filled with art materials in *C.L.O.U.D.S.* She likes to put things in her pictures that readers will notice. In a book about her brother Artie's messy room, one of her pictures shows a small garter snake intertwined in a stack of shoelaces.

When Pat Cummings is not working on one of her books, she enjoys traveling, visiting her family, going to the gym, swimming, and hanging out at the movies.

Pat Cummings

ABOUT THE AUTHOR/ILLUSTRATOR

Pat Cummings was born November 9, 1950, in Chicago. Her father was in the army (he's now a management consultant), so the family lived in many different places, never spending more than 3 years in any one place. Living in Germany put her in touch with fairy tale castles, and Okinawa left her with a sense of mysticism and tradition that helped her develop a love of fantasy. One of the books she remembers her librarian mother reading to her was a book of German fairy tales, *Tales of the Rhine*. Other books she remembers are C. S. Lewis's *Narnia Chronicles*, especially *The Lion, the Witch, and the Wardrobe*, and *A Wrinkle in Time* by Madeleine L'Engle. She doesn't remember having picture books illustrated with Black characters. And she didn't realize that her love of art would result in her someday becoming an author and illustrator of children's books. Cummings was not aware of the different career possibilities, but she knew she "wanted to be an artist simply because there was nothing else that I ever considered doing." Children's books have proven to be an ideal way to earn a living and to do what she loves to do.

In the late 1970s, she and H. Chuku Lee moved to Brooklyn, where the settled into a huge loft. At the time there were no street signs in the area and no doorbells in sight. The building Cummings and Lee live in used to be a sculpture factory. All the buildings in their neighborhood were formerly factories, and even though people, many of them artists, have been moving into them over the years, the cobblestone street still looks very deserted much of the time. Their loft overlooks the waterfront, where they can see ships coming in from all over the world. When Cummings is working at her desk, she can see all of lower Manhattan, the World Trade Center towers, and the South Street seaport—great locations for July fireworks. Actually she can watch fireworks on the seaport all summer long.

Cummings's husband, H. Chuku Lee, also has his office at home. He is a real estate appraiser and has a trade business. In his business he deals with people from all over the world, buying and selling such strange things as ginger and brake pads for construction vehicles. The phone is apt to ring with a fax at any time of the day or night.

Pat Cummings was a freelance artist for several years. She did illustration work in advertising, magazines, and newspapers. She did some illustrations for different children's theater groups in New York and was taking her portfolio around to publishers when the Council of Interracial Books for Children featured her in their "Upcoming Artists" section. That article prompted an editor to offer her a book to illustrate. Her first book, *Good News* by Eloise Greenfield, was published in 1977 by Coward, McCann & Geoghegan. Tom Feelings, a noted illustrator himself, became Cummings's mentor and guided her by giving pointers and by explaining procedures. In the next 9 years she illustrated nine more books. Some of them were written by other authors; some she authored herself. Her books are now providing readers of picture books with stories that have Black characters in them. It pleases her that the book for which she was honored with the 1984 Coretta Scott King Award, *My Mama Needs Me* by Mildred Pitts Walter (Lothrop, 1983), and the 1983 honor book, *Just Us Women* by Jeannette Caines (HarperCollins, 1982) are on subjects that appeal to all children. In Cummings's words, the stories are about "humans who happen to be Black." *Storm in the Night* and *C.L.O.U.D.S.* were also named Coretta Scott King honor books during the year following their respective publication dates (1988 and 1982).

The story in each book, according to Cummings, is what influences the medium and style she chooses for the illustrations. During a speech at a conference in Iowa City, Iowa (October 28, 1989), she said that she reads the story over and over and imagines the story pictures. Sometimes she does "about 73 variations on a page." Caines's *Just Us Women* takes place entirely in the imagination of a little girl who is planning a very special trip with her Aunt Martha. For this book Cummings chose to create realistic illustrations, and she modeled the two main characters after her sister and a niece, Keija. Her husband appears in the illustrations as one of the family members. She used black-and-white pencil to create the illustrations and actually pasted in a photocopy of an authentic road map as part of one illustration. She shaded the map to make it look folded. In this book the printer added the colors.

Cummings's favorite media and those she is most comfortable with are watercolor and colored pencil, though at one time she said she "was getting ready to use oil." A friend, illustrator Diane Dillon, has suggested she use pastels, and one of Cummings's editors encourages her to experiment, so she has used rubber stamps and collages when creating illustrations. When she gets a manuscript, she begins by reading it again and again. Once she is ready to begin the illustrating process, she makes sketches and then a dummy. Sometimes she will take photographs of people and places to use as models for some of her drawings or paintings. Later she draws a final outline. Once the drawing suits her, Cummings transfers the outline onto a watercolor paper—a fairly heavy type that won't buckle if she loads it with paint. Once the outline is transferred to the watercolor paper, she begins painting. The painting itself often takes 2 or 3 days. When she is enjoying a piece, she likes "to noodle endlessly," so sometimes the hardest part is stopping. For the illustrations for *C.L.O.U.D.S.*, Cummings used an airbrush to help achieve a continuous tone. The result is magnificent illustrations that have an iridescent, luminous effect. In a personal interview in March 1991, she said that "using pencil on top of watercolor or airbrush allows me to get layers of colors that sometime might seem to glow because your eye sees the color behind the surface color." Whatever the explanation, the result is stunning.

Cummings often draws friends and family into her books, giving the books a personal touch. Besides appearing in *Just Us Women*, her husband also appears as the painter in *Jimmy Lee Did It*, as the boss in *C.L.O.U.D.S.*, and as the father in *Willie's Not the Hugging Kind* (a book by Joyce Durham Barrett, HarperCollins, 1989). Cummings's illustrations for Mary Stolz's *Storm in the Night* (HarperCollins, 1988) brought her another Coretta Scott King honor. Cash, Cummings's cat, is included in the illustrations for Stolz's book.

Cummings has been both author and illustrator of several books. In those books she was able to go beyond the illustrations and into the story to draw in her family. One of the books, *Jimmy Lee Did It*, was written in part to get revenge on her brother Artie. The story is actually about Cummings's own brother, Artie, and her sister, Barbara. When Barbara was 4 years old she said, "Call me Angel." Everyone did. So the book stars Angel and Artie. The story is narrated by Angel. She tells about the trouble caused by Artie's imaginary friend. In the doughnut scene, the photograph is of her father. Her mother was originally supposed to flip the pancakes, but since it was the 1980s, she added a mustache to the pancake flipper to make the character the father.

C.L.O.U.D.S. gave Cummings a vehicle for drawing the aerial views she likes so much. She often watched the sky and the different cloud formations from her mother's porch in Virginia. She has also used different visual perspectives in other books. One scene in *Just Us Women* shows the rain and puddles on the ground from the perspective of one looking down. That scene also includes an unintentional visual play. Some of the raindrops are falling down and some seem to be "falling" up. Snakes slither through the grassy stalks beside the younger brother's bed in Jeannette Caines's *I Need a Lunch Box* (HarperCollins, 1988). The snake also shows up among the shoe laces in an illustration in another one of her books. In *Just Us Women* the women "stop and take pictures of all the famous statues." The bird statue shown in that book shows up once again in *C.L.O.U.D.S.*

The illustrations for each book Cummings creates offer something unique. Stolz's *Storm in the Night* took place in the dark, but Cummings managed to add a lot of color. She created the illustrations for Caines's *I Need a Lunch Box* using watercolors and rubber stamps. At one time she did color separations of her illustrations to prepare them for printing, but now her publishers take care of that aspect of the process.

A recent book, *Clean Your Room, Harvey Moon*, of which Cummings is both author and illustrator, is a thinly disguised exposé about her brother's messy room when he was young. She says, "I had to change the name to protect the guilty."

Although some of her books have messages, Cummings says that she doesn't think about messages up front, but she is aware of the responsibility of the message. She says she feels a responsibility to show children "something positive."

Cummings does not work on a set schedule. Much depends on the closeness of deadlines and the level of excitement she feels about what is happening in the painting/illustration. If necessary she can work around the clock, stopping to catnap for a while. As a freelance illustrator and author, she works whenever she needs to—using holidays, weekends, and nights to catch up on work. But at other times, when she has finished a book or has completed a painting that she is particularly pleased with, she might spend an entire day just hanging out—going to a movie perhaps. Sometimes she and Chuku manage to take time off at the same time.

Cummings has taught creative writing at Queens College and still spends a lot of time visiting schools and libraries. She always meets the "class artists"—the ones that *know* art is something they are going to do. The children ask her many questions. She has taken some of the most frequently asked questions and asked those questions of thirteen other artists: Victoria Chess, Leo Dillon, Diane Dillon, Richard Egielski, Lois Ehlert, Lisa Campbell Ernst, Tom Feelings, Steven Kellogg, Jerry Pinkney, Amy Schwartz, Lane Smith, Chris Van Allsburg, and David Wiesner. Their answers are featured in one of her newest books, *Talking with Artists* (Bradbury, 1992). Each artist (including Cummings herself) is featured in a section showing pictures of the artists—as children and as they are now—and some artwork from both their childhood and their adulthood. The children reading this book should get some idea of the world of art and how their own interests and abilities relate to those of artists now successful in the career of art/illustration. Cummings is also working on a "wonderful fairy tale" from Spain. It will be published by HarperCollins.

Pat Cummings holds a bachelor's degree in fine arts from Pratt Institute in Brooklyn, has spent time as assistant director of an art gallery, and has been an instructor at both Queensborough Community College in New York and in the graduate school of education at Queens College. However, most of her efforts and time are now focused on illustrating and writing children's books. When she is not working on a book, Cummings enjoys traveling, visiting her family, going to the gym, swimming, and going to the movies. Her favorite foods are seafood, spinach, cheese, breads, and popcorn. Her favorite color changes from time to time—but periwinkle blue is a sometimes favorite.

For those who are interested in writing or illustrating as a career, Pat Cummings has a message:

> If you are interested in writing or illustrating as a career, stick with it. It's important to show your work to people ... you have to be willing to let people see what you can do. If you have THE greatest drawings and THE best writing and you don't want others to see it you probably won't find work in those fields. But if you love art or writing, I don't think there can be any job that is more enjoyable than doing books.

It is clear that Pat Cummings's love of her work shines through in everything she creates.

THE BOOKSHELF

Cummings, Pat. **Clean Your Room, Harvey Moon.** Illustrated by Pat Cummings. Bradbury, 1991.

Socks, marbles, trains, and a map of the brain crowd the rug in Harvey's room and hide under his bed. The only way Harvey is going to get to watch cartoons is to clean his room.

1. Draw a picture of your room when it is messy. Draw a second picture showing it when it is clean.

2. Look closely at the illustrations in *Clean Your Room, Harvey Moon.* Find the snake among the shoelaces. Are there any other hidden objects in the pictures created by Pat Cummings?

3. Write a paragraph or two telling how your parents get you to clean your room.

Cummings, Pat. **C.L.O.U.D.S.** Illustrated by Pat Cummings. Lothrop, 1986.

When Pat Cummings was a young girl, she often sat on her mother's porch in Virginia and watched the clouds in the changing sky. That scene gave her the idea for this book. Chuku works for the department of *Creative Lights, Opticals,* and *Unusual Designs* in the *Sky* (C.L.O.U.D.S.). His job is to design the sky above New York.

1. Use a large sheet of paper to design a sky for over your house.

2. Read other books about clouds and weather topics.

Clouds and Weather

Bendick, Jeanne. *How to Make a Cloud.* Parents, 1971.

Branley, Franklyn M. *Flash, Crash, Rumble, and Roll.* Crowell, 1985.

Broekel, Ray. *Storms: A New True Book.* Children's, 1982.

dePaola, Tomie. *The Cloud Book.* Illustrated by Tomie dePaola. Holiday, 1975.

Lambert, David. *Weather.* Watts, 1983.

McFall, Gardner. *Jonathan's Cloud.* HarperCollins, 1986.

Rayner, Mary. *The Rain Cloud*. Atheneum, 1980.

Renberg, Dalia Hardof. *Hello, Clouds!* Illustrated by Alona Frankel. HarperCollins, 1985.

Rubin, Louis D., Sr., and Jim Duncan. *The Weather Wizard's Cloud Book*. Algonquin Books of Chapel Hill, 1984.

Shaw, Charles G. *It Looked Like Spilt Milk*. HarperCollins, 1947; Trophy, 1988.

Spier, Peter. *Dreams*. Doubleday, 1986.

Szilagyi, Mary. *Thunderstorm*. Bradbury, 1985.

Wolff, Barbara. *Evening Gray, Morning Red*. Macmillan, 1976.

3. Record the clouds/sky scene above your school or home over a period of time. Make a C.L.O.U.D. design book.

Stolz, Mary. **Go Fish.** Illustrated by Pat Cummings. HarperCollins, 1991.
   See entry in this unit for Stolz's *Storm in the Night*, page 49.

Greenfield, Eloise. **Good News.** Illustrated by Pat Cummings. Coward, 1977
   James Edward could read. He was excited to tell his mother and to read to her. But...

1. Compare the illustrations in *Good News* illustrated by Cummings with the illustrations she has created for more recent books. How do they compare in quality and technique?

2. Draw a picture of you sharing a special secret with someone in your family. Write the secret on a piece of paper and hide it somewhere in your picture.

3. Make a list of things you have learned to do since you first learned to read.

4. Make a list of all the people in your family who can read, all the people who can cook, etc.

Caines, Jeannette. **I Need a Lunch Box.** Illustrated by Pat Cummings. HarperCollins, 1988.

A young boy whose older sister, Doris, is going to get a new lunch box thinks he should have a lunch box, too, even though he isn't going to school. He thinks of all the things he could put in a lunch box, and he dreams of having a different one for every day of the school week.

1. Design a lunch box to use on each of the five school days.

2. Design a lunch box to use on your happiest day and one to use on your saddest day.

3. Make a list of things you could put in a lunch box.

4. Cummings used rubber stamps to create parts of her illustrations. Make some of your own illustrations using rubber stamps to create parts of the drawings.

Walter, Mildred Pitts. **My Mama Needs Me.** Illustrated by Pat Cummings. Lothrop, 1983.

Mother brings a new baby home from the hospital. Jason wants to help but doesn't know if his mother will need him or not.

1. Extend the focus on hugs by reading and discussing Kathleen Hague's *Bear Hugs* (Henry Holt, 1989) and David Ross's hug books cited in the entry in this unit for Barrett's *Willie's Not the Hugging Kind*, page 51.

2. Extend the theme of empathy and companionship by reading and discussing some of the following books.

Family Companionship

Aliki. *We Are Best Friends.* Illustrated by Aliki. Greenwillow, 1982.

dePaola, Tomie. *Now One Foot, Now the Other.* Illustrated by Tomie dePaola. Putnam, 1981.

Rabe, Bernice. *The Balancing Girl.* Illustrated by Lillian Hoban. Dutton, 1981.

Steptoe, John. *Stevie.* Illustrated by John Steptoe. HarperCollins, 1969.

3. Compare James's attitude about his new sister with the attitudes between siblings expressed in some of the following books.

Sibling Relationships

Bottner, Barbara. *Big Boss! Little Boss!* Pantheon, 1978.

Brown, Marc. *Arthur's Baby.* Little, Brown, 1987.

Cleary, Beverly. *Ramona and Her Mother.* Dell, 1979.

Dragonwagon, Crescent. *I Hate My Brother Harry.* Illustrated by Dick Gackenbach. HarperCollins, 1983.

Wells, Rosemary. *Don't Spill It Again, James.* Dial, 1977.

Stolz, Mary. **Storm in the Night.** Illustrated by Pat Cummings. HarperCollins, 1988.

In the dark of the night during a power outage, the sky filled with thunder and lightning, a Black grandfather tells his young grandson about a frightening storm that took place during his childhood. Cummings's illustrations were created with gouache, and even though the story takes place at night, the pictures are filled with color seen through the flashes of lightning.

1. Compare with students the text, illustrations, and mood of this book with the same elements of Arnold Adoff's *Tornado* (Delacorte, 1977) and Mary Szilagyi's *Thunderstorm* (Bradbury, 1985).

2. Grandfather's story of when he was young is similar to many of James Stevenson's stories. In several of Stevenson's books — *Grandpa's Too-Good Garden* (Greenwillow, 1989), *The Great Big Especially Beautiful Easter Egg* (Greenwillow, 1983), *That Terrible Halloween Night* (Greenwillow, 1980), *That Dreadful Day* (Greenwillow, 1985), and *There's Nothing to Do!* (Greenwillow, 1986) Grandpa recounts stories of when he was young — stories that attempt to illustrate a point to his grandchildren, Mary Ann and Louie. Information about James Stevenson and activity suggestions for the above titles are included in Sharron McElmeel's *An Author a Month (for Nickels)* (Libraries Unlimited, 1990). Students can share their grandparents' stories.

3. Grandfather and Thomas are back in another adventure in Mary Stolz's *Go Fish*, illustrated by Pat Cummings (HarperCollins, 1991). When Grandfather suggests that the two of them go fishing, Thomas is out the door in a flash, because he knows the trip will be an adventure. Grandfather is sure to have wonderful stories filled with fishing lore, tales about when dinosaurs were king, and tales of his own from Africa. Hold a roundtable discussion where students can share adventures they have had with a grandparent or older family member. Make a list of activities represented.

Cummings, Pat. **Talking with Artists.** Bradbury, 1992.

Fourteen artists — Pat Cummings, Victoria Chess, Leo Dillon, Diane Dillon, Richard Egielski, Lois Ehlert, Lisa Campbell Ernst, Tom Feelings, Steven Kellogg, Jerry Pinkney, Amy Schwartz, Lane Smith, Chris Van Allsburg, and David Wiesner — are featured. For each artist, Cummings includes a childhood picture and a recent photograph. She also includes artwork the artists created when they were children and in recent years.

1. Locate, share, and compare books illustrated by each of the artists (including Cummings).

   • Books illustrated by Victoria Chess — *The Twisted Witch and Other Spooky Riddles* by David A. Adler (Holiday, 1985); *A Little Touch of Monster* by Emily Lampert (Little, Brown, 1986); *Jim, Who Ran Away from His Nurse, and Was Eaten by a Lion* by Hilaire Belloc (Little, Brown, 1987); *The Complete Story of the Three Blind Mice* by John W. Ivimey (Joy Street, 1990); *A Hippopotamusn't: And Other Animal Verses* by J. Patrick Lewis (Dial, 1990); and *Tommy at the Grocery Store* by Bill Grossman (HarperCollins, 1989).

   • Books illustrated by Leo Dillon and Diane Dillon — *The Tale of the Mandarin Ducks* retold by Katherine Paterson (Lodestar, 1990); *Aida* retold by Leontyne Price (Gulliver, 1990); *Moses' Ark: Stories from the Bible* by Alice Bach and J. Cheryl Exum (Delacorte, 1989); *Ashanti to Zulu: African Traditions* by Margaret Musgrove (Dial, 1976); and *Why Mosquitoes Buzz in People's Ears* by Verna Aardema (Dial, 1975). (Additional titles and information about the Dillons are included in *Bookpeople: A First Album* by Sharron McElmeel [Libraries Unlimited, 1990]).

- Books illustrated by Richard Egielski—*Oh, Brother* by Arthur Yorinks (Farrar, 1989); *The Tub People* by Pam Conrad (HarperCollins, 1989); *A Telling of Tales: Five Stories* by William J. Brooke (HarperCollins, 1990); *Ugh* by Arthur Yorinks (Farrar, 1990); *It Happened in Pinsk* by Arthur Yorinks (Farrar, 1983); *Louis the Fish* by Arthur Yorinks (Farrar, 1980); *Sid and Sol* by Arthur Yorinks (Farrar, 1990); and *Hey, Al!* by Arthur Yorinks (Farrar, 1986).

- Books illustrated by Lois Ehlert—*Color Farm* by Lois Ehlert (HarperCollins, 1990); *Feathers for Lunch* by Lois Ehlert (Harcourt, 1990); *Fish Eyes: A Book You Can Count On* by Lois Ehlert (Harcourt, 1990); *Chicka Chicka Boom Boom* by Bill Martin, Jr. and John Archambault (Simon, 1989); and *Thump, Thump, Rat a Tat Tat* by Gene Baer (HarperCollins/Zolotow, 1989).

- Books authored and illustrated by Lisa Campbell Ernst—*Ginger Jumps* (Bradbury, 1990); *The Prize Pig Surprise* (Lothrop, 1984); *Gumshoe Goose, Private Eye* by Mary DeBall Kwitz (Dial, 1991); and *Sam Johnson and the Blue Ribbon Quilt* (Lothrop, 1983).

- Books illustrated by Tom Feelings—*Jambo Means Hello: Swahili Alphabet Book* by Muriel Feelings (Dial, 1974); *Moja Means One: Swahili Counting Book* by Muriel Feelings (Dial, 1972); *Daydreamers* by Eloise Greenfield and Tom Feelings (Dial, 1981); *Black Child* by Joyce Carol Thomas (Zamani Productions, 1981); and *Now Sheba Sings the Song* by Maya Angelou (Dial, 1987).

- Books illustrated by Steven Kellogg—*Jimmy's Boa and the Big Splash Birthday Bash* by Trinka Hakes Noble (Dial, 1989); *Is Your Mama a Llama?* by Deborah Guarino (Scholastic, 1989); *The Day the Goose Got Loose* by Reeve Lindbergh (Dial, 1990); *Engelbert the Elephant* by Tom Paxton (Morrow, 1990); *Appelard and Liverwurst* by Mercer Mayer (Morrow, 1978); *Liverwurst Is Missing* by Mercer Mayer (Morrow, 1981); *Pinkerton, Behave!* by Steven Kellogg (Dial, 1979); and *The Island of the Skog* by Steven Kellogg (Dial, 1973). (Additional titles and information about Steven Kellogg are included in *An Author a Month (for Pennies)* by Sharron McElmeel [Libraries Unlimited, 1989]).

- Books illustrated by Jerry Pinkney—*Home Place* by Crescent Dragonwagon (Macmillan, 1990); *Further Tales of Uncle Remus: The Misadventures of Brer Rabbit, Brer Fox, Brer Wolf, the Doodang, and Other Creatures* retold by Julius Lester (Dial, 1990); *Pretend You're a Cat* by Jean Marzollo (Dial, 1990); *The Talking Eggs: A Folktale from the American South* by Robert D. San Souci (Dial, 1989); *Turtle in July* by Marilyn Singer (Macmillan, 1989); and *In for Winter, Out for Spring* by Arnold Adoff (Harcourt, 1991).

- Books illustrated by Amy Schwartz—*The Lady Who Put Salt in Her Coffee* by Lucretia Hale, retold by Amy Schwartz (Harcourt, 1989); *Blow Me a Kiss, Miss Lilly* by Nancy White Carlstrom (HarperCollins, 1990); *Fancy Aunt Jess* by Amy Hess (Morrow, 1990); *Wanted: Warm, Furry Friend* by Stephanie Calmenson (Macmillan, 1990); *Mother Goose's Little Misfortunes* by Amy Schwartz and Leonard Marcus (Bradbury, 1990).

- Books illustrated by Chris Van Allsburg—*Swan Lake* by Mark Helprin (Houghton/Ariel, 1989); *Just a Dream* by Chris Van Allsburg (Houghton, 1990); *The Z was Zapped* by Chris Van Allsburg (Houghton, 1987); and *The Polar Express* by Chris Van Allsburg (Houghton, 1985). (Additional titles and information about Chris Van Allsburg are included in *An Author a Month (for Pennies)* by Sharron McElmeel [Libraries Unlimited, 1989]).

- Books illustrated by David Wiesner—*Hurricane* by David Wiesner (Clarion, 1990); *The Sorcerer's Apprentice* by Marianna Mayer (Bantam, 1989); *Kite Flier* by Dennis Haseley (Four Winds, 1986); *Tuesday* by David Wiesner (Clarion, 1991); and *Free Fall* by David Wiesner (Clarion, 1988).

2. Become familiar with the work of each of the artists and have students compare the artist's childhood drawings with the artist's present artwork.

3. Create a book of classroom artists. Ask each child to bring in a drawing he or she created as a younger child and then create a current work of art. Make a chapter for each child-artist following the prototype of Cummings's book. If the children are primary-aged students, perhaps an exhibit of their current work could be exhibited with a caption "Meet TODAY'S Artists."

Walter, Mildred Pitts. **Two and Too Much.** Illustrated by Pat Cummings. Bradbury, 1990.

A lively 2-year-old girl shows her 7-year-old brother more than he wants to know about her disaster-filled life.

1. Focus on the brother-sister relationship in this story and have students compare and contrast it with relationships found in some of the following titles:

Sibling Relationships

Adler, C. S. *Get Lost, Little Brother.* Clarion, 1983 (novel).

Baker, Betty. *My Sister Says.* Illustrated by Tricia Taggart. Macmillan, 1984.

Dragonwagon, Crescent. *I Hate My Brother Harry.* Illustrated by Dick Gackenbach. HarperCollins, 1983.

Hughes, Ted. "My Brother Bert." In *The Random House Book of Poetry.* Edited by Jack Prelutsky. Illustrated by Arnold Lobel. Random, 1983.

Barrett, Joyce Durham. **Willie's Not the Hugging Kind.** Illustrated by Pat Cummings. HarperCollins, 1989.

Willie allows Jo-Jo to convince him that hugging is silly, so Willie draws away from everyone who wants to hug him. Members of his family try to respect his wishes in this matter.

1. Make a list of people you would like to hug and a list of people you would like to hug you back.

2. Read David Ross's *A Book of Hugs!* (Crowell, 1982, 1986); *More Hugs!* (Crowell, 1984); and *Baby Hugs* (Crowell, 1987). Practice some of the hugs Ross describes.

3. Make a book illustrating and describing the hugs your family and friends give to one another.

FURTHER READING

Pat Cummings spent her childhood in many countries. She does not recall having had access to any picture books with Black characters. Her contribution to cultural awareness is having created illustrations for books that are about everyday happenings with everyday characters who just happen to be Black. Because of her illustrations many more children are seeing African-American people in ordinary roles in a pluralistic and multicultural American society. There are now some books other than folktales that feature Black characters doing ordinary things in a contemporary society. Among those that might be featured are *A Snowy Day* by Ezra Jack Keats (Viking, 1962; Puffin, 1976); *A Chair for My Mother* by Vera B. Williams (Greenwillow, 1982); *Stevie* by John Steptoe[1] (HarperCollins, 1969); and other titles by those authors. Locate books that depict Blacks in everyday activities and make sure some are available to students throughout the school year. Make a point to read some of those books aloud on a regular basis.

---

[1]John Steptoe and his books are featured in *An Author a Month (for Nickels)* by Sharron McElmeel (Englewood, Colo.: Libraries Unlimited, 1990).

Mem Fox

From *Bookpeople: A Multicultural Album* by Sharron L. McElmeel (Libraries Unlimited, Inc., 1992)

Mem Fox

Mem Fox was born on March 5, 1946, in Melbourne, Australia. Her birth name was Merrion Frances Partridge, but she was called "Mem" almost immediately. When Mem was 6 months old, her missionary parents, Wilfrid and Nancy Partridge, took the family to Rhodesia (now Zimbabwe), Africa. Mem lived in Africa until she was 18 and then went to England to study drama. After marrying Malcolm Fox, she returned with him to Africa to work in an organization much like the United States Peace Corps. But after a year or so, the Foxes moved to Australia.

When Mem Fox became a teacher, she also became a storyteller. She told stories on television and became a celebrity in her home country. For a class she was taking she wrote *Hush, the Invisible Mouse.* Publishers rejected the book nine times—it was "too Australian." Eventually the mouse became a possum, and the title was changed to *Possum Magic.* It is now one of Australia's best-selling books. Since then, Mem Fox has written more than twenty books. One of them has her father's name as its title, *Wilfrid Gordon McDonald Partridge.*

Mem Fox and her husband, Malcolm, and their daughter, Chloë, live in Adelaide, South Australia. Her favorite things include food from India, the color pink, and *Koala Lou* (another of her books).

Mem Fox

ABOUT THE AUTHOR

Merrion Frances Partridge was born in Melbourne, Australia, on March 5, 1946. She has been "Mem" for so long that she says her "real name doesn't sound like the real me any more." Her father, Wilfrid Gordon McDonald Partridge, and her mother, Nancy Walkden Brown Partridge, were missionaries, and when Mem was just 6 months old the family moved to Rhodesia, now Zimbabwe. She lived in Africa until 1965, when at the age of 18 she moved to England to study drama. That is where she met Malcolm Fox, whom she married on January 2, 1969. She soon returned to Africa, accompanied by her English husband, to serve in the British equivalent of the Peace Corps. Once their commitment was completed, the Foxes, lured by Australia's solicitation for immigrants, moved there in January 1970. When they arrived Mem began teaching in a Catholic girls' school, and in 1971 daughter Chloë was born. Two years later Mem became a drama lecturer at a teacher's college, the Strut Campus of the South Australian College of Advanced Education. For many years she was a senior lecturer there.

As a child Mem Fox was immersed in the language and stories of the Bible. Later in England she studied Shakespeare. From both those experiences she learned to value words and phrasing. She abandoned her acting career, but her interest in drama led her eventually to turn to storytelling. In 1978 Mem Fox founded the South Australia Storytellers Guild. She had her own storytelling television show, which made her famous throughout Australia. Her series of twelve programs have been repeated twice a year for 5 years.

As part of a university course in children's literature, Mem Fox wrote a story titled *Hush, the Invisible Mouse*, which she later sent to publishers. During the next 5 years, the book received nine rejections. Some thought the story was "too Australian." But an editor at Omnibus Books saw it and liked it but suggested that the mouse become a possum and that the title be changed to *Possum Magic*. Fox agreed to make the changes, and the book was published in 1983. During the first year, the book had to be reprinted ten times. And almost immediately Hush and Grandma Poss became the subject of all sorts of promotional items: T-shirts, stationery, buttons, calendars, bedding, pottery, and baby and birthday books. This enormous success came from Mem Fox's first book.

Part of Fox's success can surely be attributed to her awareness of the three cueing systems—semantic, syntactic, graphophonic—that children use to make sense of print. She is also acutely aware of the importance of rhythm, rhyme, and repetition as aids to reading. Very important, too, is prior knowledge (sometimes referred to as schematic background): reading one book teaches young readers how to read another. Along with the cueing systems, children must develop a knowledge of how books work. Fox also attempts to appeal to the child-within-the-parent who is reading with the child. For example, in Australia it was rather well known that the wife of the premier of Queensland, whose capital is Brisbane, is famous for her pumpkin scones, so Fox had Grandma Poss and Hush eat "pumpkin scones in Brisbane." The teacher part of Fox lets her take advantage of opportunities to include all of the Australian state capitals in her books and to make it clear that Tasmania is an island-state. For example, in *Possum Magic* she writes, "'You look wonderful, you precious possum!' said Grandma Poss. 'Next stop. Tasmania!' And over the sea they went." Non-Australian readers can gain from Fox's books some awareness of Australian geography and some knowledge of the foods and animals of Australia.

One of Mem Fox's books bears her father's name: *Wilfrid Gordon McDonald Partridge*. In that story Wilfrid Gordon McDonald Partridge is a little boy who visits a home where older residents live. The boy becomes acquainted with Miss Nancy, who has four names just like him: Nancy Alison Delacourt Cooper. Nancy is Mem's mother's name. And Alison Delacourt Cooper is a combination of her two sisters' names.

Fox writes many drafts for each of her books. For example, *Koala Lou*, which she wrote over a period of 2 years, took her forty-nine drafts, and the story was only 488 words long. *Koala Lou* began as a story that Olivia Newton-John, the Australian singer and superstar, and her partner, Pat Farrar, asked her to write. They wanted a story about a koala they could publish and market as part of the promotion of the Australian shop they had opened in Los Angeles. The name of the shop was Koala Blue, and that was the original name of the character in Fox's book. Fox developed the idea of a Koala named Koala Blue who participated in the Bush Olympics. Throughout the story, the phrase "Koala Blue I Do Love You" is used as a refrain. After the book was finished, Newton-John and Farrar decided that they did not have the resources to publish the book and returned it to Fox with the suggestion that she try to publish it elsewhere. However, she would have to change the name since that was their trademark. Finding another name that would rhyme with "you" was at first a problem. Fox rejected Koala Koo, Koala Sue, and Koala New, and finally settled on Koala Lou. It had taken 2 years to write the book and 5 years to go from "Koala Blue and the Bush Olympics" to the published *Koala Lou*. Of Fox's own books, *Koala Lou* is her favorite. That book, along with *Wilfrid Gordon McDonald Partridge*, receives the most response from readers.

All Fox's books do not take as long as *Koala Lou* however. *Hattie and the Fox* went through only four drafts and was finished in 2 days.

Since 1983, Fox has written more than twenty books, about half of which have been published in the United States. She describes writing as difficult but rewarding. Those rewards, she says, include hearing someone say, "I just *love* your books," and finding that one of her books is on the same best-seller list with *Animalia* and *The Eleventh Hour* (both books by Graeme Base, published in the U.S. by Abrams). When Mem Fox visits with schoolchildren, she is often asked about her writing and her advice for writers. The list on page 57 is based on her "Ten Hints on Writing."

Mem Fox is also acutely aware of role models in children's fiction. She often gets letters from young readers who think that the possum, Hush, is male. She's not; she is a she. But if reader after reader can assume that the "hero" of a story is a male, that distresses Mem Fox. So she has determined that she will have only female protagonists for the rest of her writing career. The only departure from that was Wilfrid Gordon McDonald Partridge in the book of the same title. That was her father's name, and she loved him and the rhythm of his name. However, even in that book she kept in mind that she is writing for boys as well as girls, so when Wilfrid Gordon asks Mr. Tippet, "What's a memory?" Mr. Tippet replies forthrightly, "Something that makes you cry, my boy, something that makes you cry." The message to young male readers is clear: it's okay to cry.

Mem and Malcolm Fox have lived in the capital of South Australia, Adelaide, since first returning to the country in 1970. Their daughter Chloe is in her early twenties and beginning her own life. The family's home is nestled in a hilly, wooded area south of Adelaide. Mem says she occasionally uses the kitchen table for writing but usually writes in the study she designed herself. It has a desk along one entire wall. She uses her word processor for final drafts but prefers to write early drafts in longhand with a 4B pencil. She writes late at night but finds it difficult to write at all when she is teaching during the academic year. Fox describes herself as "a senior lecturer in Language Arts at Flinders University, South Australia." Her work load at the university, publicity trips, and dealing with all the letters she gets — "I get millions, it seems" — takes away some of her writing time.

The Fox household includes fish, dogs, a cat, and guinea pigs. On Mem's own lists of favorites are food from India, the color pink, and two picture books: *John Brown, Rose and the Midnight Cat* by Jenny Wagner, illustrated by Ron Brooks (Puffin, 1980), and *Willy the Wimp* by Anthony Browne (Julia McRae, 1984; Knopf, 1984). And her favorite things to do when she is not working are sleeping and traveling. One day she'd like to move to a house by the beach, and she'd like one of her books to win the Children's Book Council Children's Picture Book of the Year Award. Other than those two things, she says, "I'm enormously happy with my life as it is."

Ten Hints on Writing

1. Find ideas from things that happen in your own life.

2. Don't expect the first draft to be the last draft. Good writing comes from rewriting.

3. Don't be neat at first. Neatness is dangerous: it stops you from wanting to change things. Only the final draft should be neat. Very neat!

4. Enjoy yourself. Have *fun* while you write! As you write imagine someone reading and enjoying your writing.

5. Ask friends to help you make your writing better; get them to tell you what's boring, confusing, or a waste of time so that you can change those things. Ask them if you've left out anything they'd like to know. Ask them to tell you the bits they liked best.

6. The first line, the "lead," must grab the reader.

7. The last line needs a good, smooth rhythm to satisfy the reader.

8. Read your writing aloud as you draft.

9. Interesting writing incorrectly spelled is better than boring writing correctly spelled, but all final drafts should be both interesting *and* correct. Correct writing has power. Powerful writers are powerful people. Incorrect writing is *not* acceptable in the end.

10. Writers teach themselves how to write by reading other people's writing. Read, read, read!

—Adapted from "Ten Hints on Writing" by Mem Fox, 1990.

THE BOOKSHELF

Fox, Mem. **Guess What?** Illustrated by Vivienne Goodman. Harcourt/Gulliver, 1990.

Brief questions help readers make various guesses about Daisy O'Grady. As the story unfolds, the clues make it clear that Daisy O'Grady is a witch, a hideous and scary witch. The illustrations are the most interesting part of this book, but they are also the most gruesome.

1. Use this book to stimulate a discussion about witches—good versus bad. Is there such a thing as a good witch?

2. Introduce other books featuring the witch theme. Many of the following are "gentler" titles. The Jack title gives some historical data about witches.

Witches and More Witches

Adams, Adrienne. *A Woggle of Witches.* Illustrated by Adrienne Adams. Atheneum, 1971.

Collins, Trish. *Grinkles: A Keen Halloween Story.* Watts, 1981.

Finger, Charles G. "The Hungry Old Witch." In *Witches, Witches, Witches,* compiled by Helen Hoke. Watts, 1958.

Hardendorff, Jeanne G. *Witches, Wit and Werewolf.* Lippincott, 1971.

Hutchins, Pat. *Which Witch Is Which?* Illustrated by Pat Hutchins. Greenwillow, 1989.

Jack, Adrienne. *Witches and Witchcraft.* Watts, 1980.

Johnston, Tony. *The Witch's Hat.* Illustrated by Margot Tomes. Putnam, 1984.

Fox, Mem. **Hattie and the Fox.** Illustrated by Patricia Mullins. Ashton Scholastic, 1986; Bradbury, 1986 (1987).

Hattie, the black hen, sees two eyes in the bushes, then two eyes and two ears, and eventually—"It's a fox, it's a fox." This cumulative tale invites listener participation. The story can be read again and again with the same level of delight.

1. Read it, share it, and reread it again. Be sure the listeners chime in on the refrain when the animals speak. And certainly after the first time, they will anticipate the very loud "MOOO" made by the cow when she scares the fox away.

2. Have children make their own illustrations for an animal in the bush. Then retell the story. Only this time it'll be a _____ in the bushes.

3. Provide green tissue paper bits and other paper so that children can make a torn paper collage of the bush with the fox or another animal hidden in the background.

Fox, Mem. **Koala Lou.** Illustrated by Pamela Lofts. Ian Drakeford, 1988; Harcourt/Gulliver, 1988 (1989).

Koala Lou felt that everyone loved her. Her mother loved her most of all and told her so a hundred times a day. But as Koala Lou's brothers and sisters come along, her mother is often too busy to tell her. A victory in the Bush Olympics is a chance to hear those words again. But when she comes in second....

1. Create the "play-by-play" commentary for a radio broadcast of Koala Lou's Olympic event.

2. Make a list of other events that might have been part of the Bush Olympics.

3. As a class, in small groups, or individually, discuss how young children and Koala Lou are alike and different.

Fox, Mem. **Night Noises.** Illustrated by Terry Denton. Omnibus, 1989; Harcourt/Gulliver, 1989.

It is a "wild winter's evening," and Lily Laceby, "who [is] nearly ninety" with "bones ... as creaky as floorboards at midnight," sits dozing by the fire with her very old companion dog, Butch Aggie. Noises outside the door arouse Butch Aggie, but grandmother seems undisturbed. When she is finally awakened, there is a very unexpected surprise at the door.

1. Interview your grandmother, grandfather, or some older member of your family, and write down some of that person's memories. Or you might want to tape record them for your family.

2. Describe how you would prepare a surprise birthday party for someone in your family.

3. Draw a picture of the birthday cake you would have baked for Lily Lacey.

4. Another story that deals with strange happenings on the other side of the door is *Possum Come a-Knockin'* by Nancy Van Laan, illustrated by George Booth (Knopf, 1990). Read it once and then reread it, inviting listeners to join in the refrain and to create sound effects for the knocking.

Fox, Mem. **Possum Magic.** Illustrated by Julie Vivas. Omnibus, 1983; Harcourt, 1983.

Grandma Poss makes bush magic. And this time she makes Hush invisible. But when Hush asks to be made visible again, Grandma Poss discovers that she does not have a magic formula for that. Then Grandma Poss remembers that the magic has "something to do with food. People food—not possum food." But she can't remember what, so Hush and Grandma Poss set out to find out. They travel from Adelaide to Melbourne, to Sydney, to Brisbane, to Darwin in an effort to make Hush visible again.

1. Trace the route of Hush and her Grandma Poss through the Australian countryside. Mark the towns and cities where they stopped to eat. Note that all the cities are regional capitals.

2. Make a list of foods that Hush and Grandma Poss ate. What would you eat?

3. Write about the things you would do to have fun if you were invisible. Would you go to a zoo and slide down a giraffe's back? Or would you...?

4. Mem Fox's characters, locales, and foods are very thoroughly Australian. If this story were being told in America, what type of animals would be characters in the story, what foods would hold the magic, and what places would Grandma [*shortened form of an animal's name*] and Hush visit? Retell the story with the new characters, locations, and foods.

Fox, Mem. **Shoes from Grandpa.** Illustrated by Patricia Mullins. Ashton Scholastic, 1989; Orchard, 1989 (1990).

A young girl's relatives are intent on finding garments for her to wear with the pair of shoes from Grandpa: "'I will buy you a skirt that won't show the dirt, / to go with the socks from the local shops, / to go with the shoes from Grandpa.'" Collages, similar to those Mullins used for *Hattie and the Fox*, make the text lively and enhance the movement of the cumulative story.

1. Make a paper doll and the clothes that were offered in the story to go with the shoes from Grandpa.

2. Use a catalog to pick out clothes for yourself that would go with the shoes from Grandpa. As each item is identified, list it as on an order form. Include the price and order number, the size, and other appropriate information. Add up the cost of the items that go with the shoes from Grandpa. How much does it cost to outfit one person?

3. If possible, cut out the catalog items in activity 2 and paste them onto the figure of a person you have drawn. Label the items as "blouse from Aunt Louise," or whatever is appropriate.

4. Read other stories that use the rhythmic patterns suggested by this story and "The House That Jack Built."

Books with the Rhythmic Pattern of "The House That Jack Built"

Emberley, Barbara. *Drummer Hoff.* Illustrated by Ed Emberley. Prentice, 1967.

Heilbroner, Joan. *This Is the House Where Jack Lives.* Illustrated by Aliki. Harper, 1962.

The House That Jack Built (La maison que Jacques a bâtie). Illustrated by Antonio Frasconi. Harcourt, 1958.

The House That Jack Built. Illustrated by Elizabeth Falconer. Ideals, 1990.

The House That Jack Built. Illustrated by Rodney Peppe. Delacorte, 1970.

The House That Jack Built. Illustrated by Seymour Chwast. Random, 1973.

Lobel, Arnold. *The Rose in My Garden.* Illustrated by Anita Lobel. Greenwillow, 1984.

Neitzel, Shirley. *The Jacket I Wear in the Snow.* Illustrated by Nancy Winslow Parker. Greenwillow, 1989.

Robart, Rose. *The Cake That Mack Ate.* Illustrated by Maryann Kovalski. Atlantic, 1986.

Rockwell, Anne. "The House That Jack Built." In *The Three Bears & 15 Other Stories.* Illustrated by Anne Rockwell. Crowell, 1975; Harper Trophy, 1984.

Wood, Audrey. *The Napping House.* Illustrated by Don Wood. Harcourt, 1984.

Fox, Mem. **Wilfrid Gordon McDonald Partridge.** Illustrated by Julie Vivas. Omnibus, 1983; Kane-Miller, 1983 (1985).

Wilfrid is a young boy who finds himself visiting a nursing home, where he becomes acquainted with Nancy Alison Delacourt Cooper, an elderly woman he calls Miss Nancy. But Miss Nancy has lost her memory, so Wilfrid sets out to find it. But first he must find out what memory is.

1. Explain what memory is. Be creative.

2. Write a letter to a person in a nursing home, or if you can, visit a nursing home and read to someone there. Ask residents to share their memories; record them.

3. Fill a box with five objects that bring back memories to you. Explain the significance.

4. Pretend that you are going to rename yourself with four names when you reach the age of 18. Use name books (those often used when parents are searching for new baby names) to choose the four names you would give yourself. Write a paragraph explaining how you came to choose those names.

5. Because Mem Fox could see the teaching possibilities in rhyme, she wanted to have the characters in the story be "Mrs. Morgan who played the organ," "Mrs. Hicks who walked with wooden sticks," and "Mr. Bryant who had a voice like a giant." But the publisher did not agree, so in the book Mrs. Jordan plays the organ, Mr. Tippet is crazy about cricket, and so on. The publisher thought rhyming names were beyond the realm of reality. Brainstorm a list of names Mem Fox could have used if the publisher had permitted her to use rhyming names. (One author who has used rhyming names very successfully is Barbara Emberley, in *Drummer Hoff*, illustrated by Ed Emberley [Prentice, 1967].)

FURTHER READING

Mem Fox's books reflect "Australianism" while appealing to the universality of deeply felt emotions. By reading books like Fox's that reflect other cultures and other countries, readers are reminded of the similarities among peoples throughout the world, despite the differences in their everyday lives. In *Hattie and the Fox*, the barnyard animals are exactly as in the United States. And even though *Possum Magic* mentions several foods that would not be readily recognized by most American readers, Mem Fox says that certain breakfast fare, especially cereals such as Cheerios® and corn flakes (sometimes Frosted Flakes® and Fruity Pebbles®) would be "as in America, exactly." Share some of the Australian foods that Fox mentions in *Possum Magic*. Then discuss the things that are the same in each country. Research and investigate animals that live in Australia, learn about the geography of the continent, investigate the relationship of winter/summer in Australia to our seasons (especially as they affect the school year), and discuss how life might be different for an American who moved to Australia.

Paul Goble

From *Bookpeople: A Multicultural Album* by Sharron L. McElmeel (Libraries Unlimited, Inc., 1992)

Paul Goble

Paul Goble was born on September 27, 1933, in England, where he grew up in a home filled with music. As a young boy, Paul Goble filled scrapbooks with pictures of Indians he cut from magazines. He read about Indians and became interested in all things Native American. His mother often read him stories of Grey Owl and Ernest Thompson Seton. He continued to be a keen student of nature and of Native Americans throughout his college and military days. His first career was as an industrial engineer, but his hobby continued to be the study of Native Americans.

In 1969 Paul Goble's first book, *Red Hawk's Account of Custer's Last Battle*, was published. Since then he has written more than eighteen books, all of them about the Plains Indians. When he moved to the United States in 1977, he became a full-time author and illustrator. Some of his recent books are about a Plains Indian trickster, Iktomi.

Paul Goble and his wife live in Lewiston, New York; their son, Robert, attends boarding school in Canada.

Paul Goble

ABOUT THE AUTHOR/ILLUSTRATOR

Paul Goble was born on September 27, 1933, in Haslemere, England. His father, Robert John Goble, was a professional harpsichord maker, and his mother, Marion Elizabeth, was a professional musician and painter. She often read stories to him, including stories by Grey Owl[1] and Ernest Thompson Seton.[2] Goble spent hours studying nature and Indians. He cut out pictures of Indians from magazines and books and collected them into scrapbooks. His mother made him an Indian outfit (fringed shirt, leggings, and war bonnet), which he wore as he walked around his suburban neighborhood in England. His parents encouraged both his study of Indians and his interest in art. Many of his drawings were of Indians. When he was 12, Paul moved with his family to Oxford, where he attended boarding school during the week and bicycled home to the country on the weekends. As a teenager Goble read *Black Elk Speaks*,[3] a famous autobiography of a visionary Sioux healer. He also met Joseph Epes Brown, a man who had recorded Black Elk's account of the sacred rites of the Sioux in a book titled *The Sacred Pipe*.[4] After completing school Goble spent 2 years in the military in Germany, where he was able to go horseback riding whenever he wanted, in the Hartz mountains.

In 1956, at the age of 23, Goble entered Central School of Arts and Crafts in London, where he met his first wife, Dorothy. During the summer of 1959, he was able to spend the summer on reservations in South Dakota and Montana. He eventually became an adopted member of the Yakima and Sioux tribes, and was given the name Wakinyan Chikala, "Little Thunder," by Chief Edgar Red Cloud, an Oglala Sioux and the great-grandson of the famous war chief.

Upon returning to England, Goble and his wife ran their own industrial design practice while Paul also served as a lecturer at design schools. His furniture designs won several awards. In the 1960s Goble began to search for books about Indians for his two children, Richard and Julia. Suitable books were difficult to find, because much that had been written presented misconstrued information about Native Americans, and the stories were told almost entirely from the perspective of the non-Indians who had intruded on Indian lands. After seeing a television serial about General Custer, a serial that Goble thought glorified the military, Goble decided to write an account of the battle. That account told the story from the Native-American perspective. *Red Hawk's Account of Custer's Last Battle: The Battle of the Little Big Horn*

---

[1]Grey Owl (1888-1939) was the pseudonym of George Stansfeld Belaney, an author and wildlife lecturer. He lived the life of a Canadian Indian and wrote about the wildlife he saw. His identity was not generally known during his lifetime. He claimed to have been born in Mexico, but it is believed that he was actually born in Hastings, England. His books, movies, and lectures made him famous in the 1930s, especially in England.

[2]Ernest Thompson Seton was the pseudonym of Ernest Seton Thompson, a popular writer and illustrator of animal and woodcraft books for boys. He was active in founding the Boy Scouts of America and wrote the first Boy Scout manual. He was born in South Shields, England, but spent his boyhood in Canada. Although he studied art in England, he spent his adult life in Canada and eventually lived in New York City.

[3]Black Elk, *Black Elk Speaks: Being the Life Story of a Holy Man of the Oglala Sioux* (New York: Pocket Books, 1959 [1972]; Lincoln: University of Nebraska, 1961).

[4]Joseph Epes Brown, ed. *The Sacred Pipe: Black Elk's Account of the Seven Rites of the Oglala Sioux.* (Norman: University of Oklahoma Press, 1989).

25 June 1876 was published in 1969. The author credits were shared by Goble and his wife, Dorothy, although Dorothy viewed her role as one of adviser and encourager. Goble continued to visit the United States during the summer months, often bringing his son Richard with him. Together they camped in the Black Hills of South Dakota and visited national parks, forests, and reservation areas. Goble was able to make several trips to the northern plains of the United States, where he visited with Sioux, Crow, Shoshoni, and other Plains Indian tribes. During those visits, Paul took part in ceremonies, helped build the Sun Dance lodge, and observed the sacred Sun Dances. Paul Goble and Dorothy Goble shared credit for the authorship of two more books: *Brave Eagle's Account of the Fetterman Fight, 21 December 1866* (Pantheon, 1969; University of Nebraska Press, 1992) and *Lone Bull's Horse Raid* (Macmillan, 1973). All three books were illustrated by Paul Goble. He studied the historical records Indians painted on buffalo robes. He attempted to emulate the style, using a magnifying glass to bring as much precision to his paintings as possible. His style of illustration is sometimes referred to as "Indian ledger book painting."

In 1977, Goble moved to the Black Hills of South Dakota to establish permanent residence in the United States. His marriage to Dorothy ended, and in 1978 he married Janet Tiller. For 13 years Goble lived in the Black Hills working in a small room, his "studio." All but one side of his room had windows from which he could see pine trees, the meadow, and the forest wildlife. Not waiting for inspiration, Goble would sit down every day after breakfast and begin work. For breaks he often took trips to meet with Indians on reservations, attend ceremonies, and visit historical museums around the country. His home was close to the Crow and Cheyenne reservations to the west in Montana, and to Sioux reservations to the north and east. In the museums, he studied historical Indian paintings and old Indian beadwork. And while driving through the countryside, he often stopped to view the flowers or to identify birds. He recorded his observations so that he could use certain details in his paintings. Rather than glorify or romanticize the image of animals and birds, he has always wanted simply to promote respect for all beings.

Goble creates his artwork with India ink and watercolor. His technique produces a flat appearance much like that of Indian paintings that were created by artists who made no attempt to achieve perspective and shading. Goble applies the brightly colored watercolors in layers and leaves a white thin line between the black outline and the colored inlay to suggest brilliantly colored bead and quill work. Goble thoroughly researches his topics and his artwork. He explains in the author's notes for his books the background and sources for his stories. And although Goble is serious about returning to Native-American children pride in their cultural heritage, he strives also to insert a few light touches into his illustrations. In his tales about Iktomi, Goble manages to bring the trickster from the past into the present by featuring Iktomi in jogging clothes. In one scene Iktomi is seen hanging upside down from a tree branch wearing a T-shirt that declares, "I'm Sioux and Proud of It."

Among the various awards Goble has received for his books was the Caldecott Medal in 1979 for his illustrations for *The Girl Who Loved Wild Horses*. A great number of his paintings have been used on book jackets and made into prints and notecards.

Goble's legacy to Native Americans are their own stories that he has preserved for their children. He believes that Indians and non-Indians alike need to have a knowledge and respect for the culture and history of the Native American—a culture that allowed people to live in harmony with nature.

Paul Goble now lives in Lewiston, New York, with his wife, Janet. Their teenage son, Robert, attends boarding school in Canada.

THE BOOKSHELF

Goble, Paul. **Beyond the Ridge.** Illustrated by Paul Goble. Bradbury, 1989.

When an Indian grandmother goes "beyond the ridge," she has actually gone from this life to the next. This portrayal of an Indian family dealing with the loss illustrates the tradition of allowing the body to return to the earth.

1. Another story of Indian tradition dealing with death is Miska Miles's *Annie and the Old One*, illustrated by Peter Parnall (Little, 1971). Have students discuss the two books in relation to customs in different tribes and local customs dealing with death in your community. Hospice programs and wakes are among the topics that can be part of this discussion.

2. Another theme in both Goble's book and Miles's *Annie and the Old One* is the feeling of love family members have for older relatives. To extend the theme, introduce students to some of the following books.

Family Relationships

Clark, Ann Nolan. *To Stand against the Wind.* Viking, 1978. (Vietnamese)

Flournoy, Valerie. *The Patchwork Quilt.* Illustrated by Jerry Pinkney. Dial, 1985. (African-American)

Mathis, Sharon Bell. *The Hundred Penny Box.* Illustrated by Leo Dillon and Diane Dillon. Viking, 1975; Puffin, 1986. (African-American)

Goble, Paul, and Dorothy Goble. **Brave Eagle's Account of the Fetterman Fight, 21 December 1866.** Illustrated by Paul Goble. Pantheon, 1969; University of Nebraska Press, 1992.

Sometimes referred to as "Red Cloud's War," this battle is the only instance in the history of the United States in which the federal government went to war and ended up ceding to the enemy everything it demanded. The battle took place on the Bozeman Trail in northern Wyoming between Fort Laramie, Wyoming, and Virginia City, Idaho. The battle, fought over control of the Bozeman Trail, was a triumph for Red Cloud.

1. Use the map on the endpapers of the book to identify the present-day location of the setting. Research how the area has changed over the past 130 years. Make a map of the present-day area for comparison.

2. Read more information about Red Cloud of the Oglala Sioux. An excellent source is *Indian Chiefs* by Russell Freedman (Holiday, 1987), pages 10-27. Red Cloud died in 1909.

Goble, Paul. **Buffalo Woman.** Illustrated by Paul Goble. Bradbury, 1984.

This is a transformation tale focusing on the bond between humans and buffalo herds and the Plains Indians' dependency on the buffalo. It is the story of an Indian man who marries a female buffalo that has assumed the form of an Indian maiden. Both are rejected by the Buffalo Nation. The brave must pass various tests before he is allowed to join his wife and son as a buffalo.

1. The bond between buffalo herds and humans was essential if both were to survive. This element is also emphasized in Olaf Baker's *Where the Buffaloes Begin* (Warne, 1981). Stephen Gammell's black-and-white drawings add to the mystique of the legend. Help students compare the motif of Baker's tale to the motifs in *Buffalo Woman.*

2. Focus on the element of transformation and discuss with students the similarities of transformation in tales from various cultures.

Tales of Transformation

Cleaver, Elizabeth. *The Enchanted Caribou.* Illustrated by Elizabeth Cleaver. Atheneum, 1985.

Crompton, Anne Eliot. *The Winter Wife.* Illustrated by Robert Andrew Parker. Little, Brown, 1975.

Harris, Christie. "The Prince Who Was Taken Away by the Salmon." In *Once More upon a Totem.* Illustrated by Douglas Tait. Atheneum, 1973.

McDermott, Gerald. *Arrow to the Sun: A Pueblo Indian Tale.* Illustrated by Gerald McDermott. Viking, 1974.

Perrault, Charles. *Cinderella.* Illustrated by Errol LeCain. Bradbury, 1972.

Schoolcraft, Henry Rowe. *The Ring in the Prairie: A Shawnee Legend.* Edited by John Bierhorst. Illustrated by Leo Dillon and Diane Dillon. Dial, 1970.

Yagawa, Sumiko. *The Crane Wife.* Translated by Katherine Paterson. Illustrated by Suekichi Akaba. Morrow, 1981.

Goble, Paul. **Death of the Iron Horse.** Illustrated by Paul Goble. Bradbury, 1987.

The only time a train wreck was actually caused by Indians occurred on August 7, 1867. This is a fictionalized account of the encounter between the Cheyenne and the iron horse that threatened the Native Americans' very existence. The wreck occurred when a Union Pacific freight train was traveling from Omaha to Fort McPherson (North Platte, Nebraska).

1. Use the catalog in your school or public library to locate more information about the development of the train and its importance in the non-Indian settlement of the West. Use the subject headings LOCOMOTIVES and RAILROADS.

2.   On a present-day map, locate the route between Omaha and North Platte, Nebraska. Is there a major road or railroad track between those two locations today? How did the early railroad routes affect the development of roads and the growth of settlements into towns and cities?

Goble, Paul. **Dream Wolf.** Illustrated by Paul Goble. Bradbury, 1990.

   While the wolf is often portrayed as mean and menacing in the folklore of other cultures, in the legends of Native Americans, the wolf is honored and revered. This tale tells how the wolf comes to the aid of two young children, Tiblo and Tanksi, who are lost, cold, tired, and hungry. *Dream Wolf* is based on a story originally published as *The Friendly Wolf*, coauthored by Paul Goble and Dorothy Goble, illustrated by Paul Goble (Macmillan, 1974). The original artwork appears in this revised edition, but the text has been rewritten and the cover artwork revised.

1.   Search for legends that feature wolves. Compare how the animal is portrayed in the different tales. Some wolf tales include "Little Red Riding Hood," *Lon Po Po: A Chinese Red Riding Hood Tale* by Ed Young (Philomel, 1989), and "The Three Little Pigs."

2.   Write a paragraph or a poem about the character of a wolf.

Goble, Paul. **The Gift of the Sacred Dog.** Illustrated by Paul Goble. Bradbury, 1980.

   This book focuses on the arrival of the horse (the sacred dog) and its contribution to the changing ways of the Native-American nomadic buffalo tribes that lived on the plains of the central United States.

1.   This is one of the tales that tell of how animals have assisted human beings. Read Paul Goble's *Dream Wolf* (Bradbury, 1990) and *The Great Race* (Bradbury, 1985). Compare the story line to that of *The Gift of the Sacred Dog*.

2.   Share the Reading Rainbow® program (a public television program) of *The Gift of the Sacred Dog*. Program information is distributed by the Great Plains National Instructional Television Library.

Goble, Paul. **The Girl Who Loved Wild Horses.** Illustrated by Paul Goble. Bradbury, 1978.

   This literary tale is not one legend but a combination of many. The girl loves horses and wants to ride with them. The message is fairly straightforward: our wishes and dreams can come true if our thoughts are persistent enough. In the illustrations for this book, Goble attempts to represent the sun as well as the understanding and brotherhood that the Indians feel. In the half-title page for this book, the line defining the horse's neck is shown to be part of the sun's inner circle—representing the harmony between animals and nature. Later, at the end of the story, two horses are shown with the lines defining their necks again, appearing to be part of the sun's inner circle. Goble received the 1979 Caldecott Award for this book.

1.   Compare the relationship between human beings and animals in this tale with that in Goble's *Buffalo Woman*.

2.   After reading this story, reread it, and ask listeners to record descriptive phrases—metaphors and similes—that are particularly pleasing to them. Some they choose might include: the stallion's eyes are

"cold stars," his floating mane and tail are "wispy clouds," and horses gallop "faster and faster, pursued by thunder and lightning," "like a brown flood across hills and through valleys."

3. Native Americans have a variety of legends that explain why various things occur in nature. One such legend is retold by Tomie dePaola in *The Legend of the Bluebonnet* (Putnam, 1983). The legend is the story of a Comanche girl who after sacrificing her warrior doll to bring rain to her people, brings them the bluebonnet flower. Discuss what would be an ultimate sacrifice for the students.

Goble, Paul. **The Great Race.** Illustrated by Paul Goble. Bradbury, 1985.

This is a literary version of a Cheyenne and Sioux legend of the great race for supremacy run by the Buffalo Nation and humans. The pages burst with color and vibrancy. During his period of residency in the Black Hills, Goble lived in a valley reached by Nemo Route, near Deadwood, South Dakota. Some say that was where the legendary Great Race took place.

1. Compare the theme of the story with that of *The Gift of the Sacred Dog.* Both focus on the assistance animals have given human beings. Share stories of when pets have helped humans.

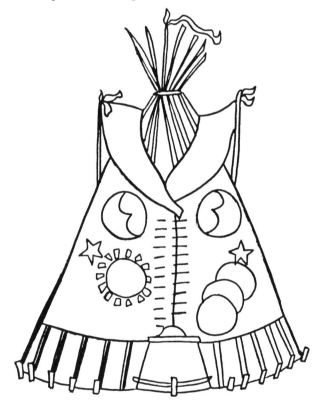

2. Goble attempts to impart information about Native Americans through his art. For example, to show how tipi design reflects the cosmos, he places the stars above and the rolling plains below—and the life-giving animals in the middle. Sun-rainbow circles symbolize the sun and the harmony of the circle of life. Many aspects of the Plains Indians are symbolized in Goble's paintings. Discuss how the illustrations for *The Great Race* embody the traditions of Native American people and how those illustrations relate to the illustrations in some of Goble's other books.

Goble, Paul. **Her Seven Brothers.** Illustrated by Paul Goble. Bradbury, 1988.

A young girl uses porcupine quills to decorate the shirts and moccasins she is making for her seven brothers—brothers she has not yet seen. The girl mysteriously knows that she must travel to the north country to find those brothers. This is a legend telling why the seven stars of the Big Dipper are in the northern sky.

1. Read other tales about how constellations came to be, and have students discuss the blend of religious beliefs in those tales, how-and-why explanations, and references to Indian custom.

Origin of the Stars

de Wit, Dorothy, ed. "What Happened to Six Wives Who Ate Onions." In *The Talking Stone: An Anthology of Native American Tales and Legends.* Illustrated by Donald Crews. Greenwillow, 1979.

Goble, Paul. *Star Boy.* Illustrated by Paul Goble. Bradbury, 1983.

Grinnell, George B. "Star Boy." In *North American Legends.* Edited by Virginia Haviland. Illustrated by Ann Strugnell, Collins, 1979.

Mobley, Jane. *The Star Husband.* Illustrated by Anna Vojtech. Doubleday, 1979.

Rockwell, Anne. *The Dancing Stars: An Iroquois Legend.* Illustrated by Anne Rockwell. Crowell, 1972.

San Souci, Robert D. *The Legend of Scarface: A Blackfeet Indian Tale.* Illustrated by Daniel San Souci. Doubleday, 1978.

Schoolcraft, Henry Rowe. *The Ring in the Prairie: A Shawnee Legend.* Edited by John Bierhorst. Illustrated by Leo Dillon and Diane Dillon. Dial, 1970.

2. Write pourquoi stories of how a specific constellation came to be.

Goble, Paul. **Iktomi and the Berries.** Orchard, 1989. **Iktomi and the Boulder.** Orchard, 1988. **Iktomi and the Buffalo Skull.** Orchard, 1991. **Iktomi and the Ducks.** Orchard, 1990.

Iktomi (eek-TOE-me) is a Sioux name for a trickster character that is the hero of many amusing stories. He is charaterized as being very clever and as having unusual magical powers, but he is also very stupid, untruthful, and mischievous. He often tries to outsmart others but generally ends up being outsmarted. Goble has done what Native-American storytellers do with these trickster tales; the storyteller, knowing that there is no correct version of the stories, is careful to keep to certain familiar themes and to weave variations of the theme into a story. The story has a moral but is not didactic in the sense that it gives a sermon. All Iktomi stories start the same way, "Iktomi was walking along…," implying to the reader that Iktomi is more interested in making mischief than in doing any useful work.

1. *Iktomi and the Buffalo Skull* emphasizes the problems that result from sticking one's nose into others' business. *Iktomi and the Boulder* explains why bats have flattened faces and why there are rocks scattered all over the Great Plains. Have students summarize, in one sentence, the basic plot of the other Iktomi books.

2. In the Iktomi books, Goble shows Iktomi to be both a character from the past and a character of the present. For example, in *Iktomi and the Boulder*, one of the final illustrations shows Iktomi in his tattered, but elaborately beaded, traditional dress, with one leg bare except for a modern-day gym sock. He also wears a baseball cap with the initial "U.S." partially visible. Look at the illustrations in the other Iktomi books and identify other examples of Iktomi in the present. Discuss with students possible reasons for Goble to include those modern touches. How would students similarly portray historical figures such as Abraham Lincoln and Benjamin Franklin?

Goble, Paul, and Dorothy Goble. **Red Hawk's Account of Custer's Last Battle: The Battle of the Little Big Horn 25 June 1876.** Illustrated by Paul Goble. Pantheon, 1969; reissued University of Nebraska Press, 1992.

After the battle at Little Big Horn, the narrator, a Native-American boy, realizes that although the battle's victory belonged to the Indians, the victory in the Indians' fight against the white invasion would ultimately belong to the white man. The Battle of Little Big Horn was the worst defeat ever suffered by the U.S. Army in a battle with Indians. It was much worse than the Fetterman fight that had occurred 10 years earlier.

1. Read more information about George Armstrong Custer in Russell Freedman's book *Indian Chiefs* (Holiday, 1987), pages 114-39.

2. Compare the statistics of the Fetterman Fight with the Battle of the Little Big Horn.

3. Compare and contrast this account of the battle with Quentin Reynolds's *Custer's Last Stand* (Random, 1951; 1987) or with the accounts contained in the following books about Sitting Bull.

Sitting Bull

Black, Sheila. *Sitting Bull.* Native American Series. Silver, 1989.

Hook, Jason. *Sitting Bull and the Plains Indians.* Life and Times Series. Watts, 1987.

Smith, Kathie Billingslea. *Sitting Bull: Tatanka Yotanka.* Illustrated by James Seward. Great American Series. Messner, 1987.

Goble, Paul. **Star Boy.** Illustrated by Paul Goble. Bradbury, 1983.

This story explains why the Sun Dance was given to the Blackfeet Indians. Because of his mother's disobedience, Star Boy is marked with a scar and must journey to the sun to have the scar removed.

1. Compare Star Boy's journey to the sun to the boy's journey to the sun as recounted in Gerald McDermott's retelling of the Pueblo legend *Arrow to the Sun: A Pueblo Indian Tale* (Viking, 1974).

2. Compare Star Boy's tale as told by Goble to versions of the tale told in other books. Goble's retelling is based on the original story collected by Grinnell. See comparison notes following the booklist.

Blackfoot Legend of Scarface/Star Husband

Grinnell, George B. "Star Boy." In *North American Legends.* Edited by Virginia Haviland. Illustrated by Ann Strugnell. Collins, 1979.

Mobley, Jane. *The Star Husband.* Illustrated by Anna Vojtech. Doubleday, 1979.

San Souci, Robert D. *The Legend of Scarface: A Blackfeet Indian Tale.* Illustrated by Daniel San Souci. Doubleday, 1978.

Comparison Notes: Star Boy — Scarface — Star Husband

Native-American stories most often combine religious beliefs, how-and-why explanations, and references to Indian customs. Goble authentically represents the Blackfeet artistic tradition through his beautiful illustrations. Star Boy is expelled with his mother. He is marked by a facial scar and becomes known as Scarface. In order to marry, he must travel to the sun to have the scar removed. To commemorate the gesture, the Blackfeet have a Sun Dance each summer. Star Boy becomes another star and joins his father, Morning Star, and his mother, Evening Star. Mobley's retelling varies in that she tells the story of a young Indian woman who wishes for a star husband. She is granted her wish, marries, and bears a boy child. When she ignores a warning to never dig in the floor of the sky, she finds that she must leave her star husband and her son, the moon. When she dies she is allowed to rejoin them in the sky, where she becomes a shining star close by the moon. The San Souci version does not refer to an original source other than to say that it is a Blackfeet legend. The illustrations in his tale are very striking, but the tale has been criticized for its heavily embroidered retelling.

FURTHER READING

Paul Goble came to write books about the Native American out of a deep interest and respect for Native-American culture. Byrd Baylor is another non-Native American who has developed a great deal of respect for the Native-American life-style. Locate books by Baylor and extend the appreciation of Native-American values as they reflect an affinity to nature and a respect for wildlife. Some titles by Baylor include *And It Is Still That Way: Legends Told by Arizona Indian Children* (Scribner, 1976), *When Clay Sings* (Scribner, 1972), *The Way to Start a Day* (Scribner, 1978), *Desert Voices* (Scribner, 1981), *Before You Came This Way* (Dutton, 1969), *Everybody Needs a Rock* (Scribner, 1974), *Guess Who My Favorite Person Is* (Aladdin, 1977), *Hawk, I'm Your Brother* (Scribner, 1976), *If You Are a Hunter of Fossils* (Scribner, 1980), *I'm in Charge of Celebrations* (Scribner, 1986), *The Other Way to Listen* (Scribner, 1978), *Your Own Best Secret Place* (Scribner, 1979), and *Moon Song* (Scribner, 1982).

Jamake Highwater

From *Bookpeople: A Multicultural Album* by Sharron L. McElmeel (Libraries Unlimited, Inc., 1992)

Jamake Highwater

Jamake Highwater introduces himself by saying that he is an American Indian, part Blackfeet and part Cherokee, that he began college at age 13 in Berkeley, California, and that he earned a doctorate in anthropology at the age of 20. Then he stops and says, "All of it is fiction; I don't know where or when I was born."

The fact is that Jamake Highwater is not altogether sure of his own heritage. Usually he says that he was born February 14, 1942 (the year is correct, he says, but the date is an estimation), in Glacier County, Montana. His Cherokee father, Jamie Highwater, was a founder of the American Indian Rodeo Association. He became a movie stuntman and took Jamake to California, where they lived out of the back of a pickup truck. After his father was killed in a car accident, Jamake Highwater was raised by the family of his father's best friend. He entered the University of California at Berkeley at a very young age and earned degrees from there and a Ph.D. from the University of Chicago. He says he speaks (and is able to joke in) eleven languages. He has homes in New York City, Turkey, and Zurich, Switzerland, where he was at one time an artist-in-residence for the Swiss government. He received the Newbery Award in 1978 for *Anpao: An American Indian Odyssey*. He has written numerous adult short stories and novels in addition to works for younger readers.

Jamake Highwater

ABOUT THE AUTHOR

The facts Highwater gives about his life are as colorful as his life itself. He says that he lived with the Blackfeet and Cree tribes in Montana and southern Canada for the first 13 years of his life, but he is not enrolled in any tribe. However, as an adult he was given the name of Piitai Sahomaapii, meaning "Eagle Son." The name ceremony was held at Lethbridge University in Alberta, Canada, when Ed Calf Robe, an elder of the Blood Reserve of Blackfeet Indians conferred a new name upon him in recognition of his achievements on behalf of Indian people. His book *Anpao: An American Indian Odyssey* is the only book about Native Americans to receive the Newbery Award. He seems very proud to be part of the American-Indian culture and tends to emphasize culture differences in order to promote understanding. In *Many Smokes, Many Moons: A Chronology of American Indian History through Indian Art* Highwater says, "We are finding different kinds of 'truths' that make the world we live in far bigger than we ever dreamed it could be—for the greatest distance between people is not geographical space but culture."[1]

Earlier in his career, Highwater was a rather more flamboyant personality than he appears to be in the 1990s. During an interview session with Sarah Crichton for *Publisher's Weekly*, Highwater was, according to Crichton's description, "an extremely handsome Indian, with chiseled features, longish black hair, warm-colored skin and perfect white teeth."[2] Crichton described his New York studio and office as being "packed with a wealth of Indian artifacts: paintings, pottery, headdresses, even a cow skull. Highwater himself was drenched in artifacts. To be precise: nine turquoise and silver necklaces; two three-inch-wide silver bracelets; three rings on each hand. A silver thunderbird hung from his black leather vest; his skin-tight jeans were topped with an impressive silver belt buckle. Only the bottom mother-of-pearl button on his red 'cowboy' shirt was fastened." He often wears an eagle feather in his hair.

While some people have questioned the authenticity of Highwater's Native-American heritage, most literary critics agree that Jamake Highwater is extremely talented and that he has brought literature about Native Americans into the mainstream. The historical and cultural merit and the integrity of his work are unimpeachable.

American School Publishers have created a filmstrip/cassette, *Meet the Newbery Author: Jamake Highwater*, that presents historic photographs of Highwater's Blackfeet ancestors. Highwater is also shown writing in the predawn hours.

---

[1]Jamake Highwater, *Many Smokes, Many Moons: A Chronology of American Indian History through Indian Art* (Lippincott, 1978), 14.

[2]Susan Crichton, "PW Interviews: Jamake Highwater," *Publisher's Weekly* (November 6, 1978): 6-8.

THE BOOKSHELF

Highwater, Jamake. **Anpao: An American Indian Odyssey.** Illustrated by Fritz Scholder. Lippincott, 1977.

Highwater says that his character Anpao is indeed a fabrication, that there is no such central Indian hero. Anpao was created as a literary device to tell the saga of Indian life in America. The novel *Anpao: An American Indian Odyssey* is a linking of old tales. Anpao, because of his love for the beautiful Ko-ko-mik-e-is, must undertake the dangerous quest of going to the house of the sun to ask that the sun remove the scar from his face. That would be a signal that the two young people could marry. Within this quest are woven various mythological tales with motifs common to folklore in the Native-American culture. The moral tone of the stories reflects Indian tradition and provides an interesting comparison and contrast to stories of other cultures. American School Publishers has a filmstrip/cassette adaptation, *Anpao: An American Indian Odyssey*, of this tale. The filmstrip is illustrated with photography that brings life and authenticity to the setting.

1. The Blackfeet legend of Scarface forms the skeleton for Anpao's odyssey. Highwater lets Anpao meet many traditional Indian characters—Coyote, Grandmother Spider, Raven, and the mouse people—as he journeys to the sun. Parts of the journey are appropriate to read aloud to middle schools students who are familiar with the outline of the story.

    a. Read a picture-book edition of the legend of Scarface as an introductory activity to this novel.

Blackfoot Legend of Scarface

Goble, Paul. *Star Boy.* Illustrated by Paul Goble. Bradbury, 1983.

Grinnell, George B. "Star Boy." In *North American Legends.* Edited by Virginia Haviland. Illustrated by Ann Strugnell. Collins, 1979.

San Souci, Robert D. *The Legend of Scarface: A Blackfeet Indian Story.* Illustrated by Daniel San Souci. Doubleday, 1978.

    b. Introduce *Anpao: An American Indian Odyssey.* Explain the premise of the story and its plot.

    c. Read aloud selected stories from within the tale, or if appropriate to the age group, read the novel in its entirety. (Some of the traditional characters in the journey are also found in other Native-American stories. For example, the mouse people are part of *Iktomi and the Buffalo Skull* by Paul Goble [see index].)

Highwater, Jamake. **Moonsong Lullaby.** Illustrated by Marcia Keegan. Lothrop, 1981.

Several themes are part of this gentle Native-American poem, including the night life of animals and plants and the moon's progress across the sky.

1. This is perhaps one of those books that should be read aloud and simply left to "shimmer in the air."

2. Extend the subject of Native-American poetry by reading some of the following.

Poetry of Nature

Baylor, Byrd. *The Desert Is Theirs.* Illustrated by Peter Parnall. Scribner, 1975.

Baylor, Byrd. *Moon Song.* Illustrated by Ronald Himler. Scribner, 1982.

Bierhorst, John, ed. *The Sacred Path: Spells, Prayers & Power Songs of the American Indians.* Morrow, 1983.

Sneve, Virginia Driving Hawk, selector. *Dancing Teepees: Poems of American Indian Youth.* Illustrated by Stephen Gammell. Holiday, 1989.

FURTHER READING

Jamake Highwater brings to his writings a respect for the Native American and tells his stories from the perspective of the Native American. Two other authors featured in this book, Paul Goble and Virginia Driving Hawk Sneve, also write stories centering on Native-American culture. Identify common themes and characters as they appear in the work of various authors who write about Native Americans. In addition to the titles by Goble and Sneve, the following books should be available in established libraries. Read widely from this list, and use the stories to encourage class discussion.

Native-American Literature

Crompton, Anne Eliot. *The Winter Wife.* Illustrated by Robert Andrew Parker. Little, Bown, 1975.

Grinnell, George B. *The Whistling Skeleton: American Indian Tales of the Supernatural.* Edited by John Bierhorst. Illustrated by Robert Andrew Parker. Four Winds, 1982.

Harris, Christie. *Mouse Woman and the Mischief-Makers.* Illustrated by Douglas Tait. Atheneum, 1977.

_____. *Mouse Woman and the Muddleheads.* Illustrated by Douglas Tait. Atheneum, 1979.

_____. *Mouse Woman and the Vanished Princess.* Illustrated by Douglas Tait. Atheneum, 1976.

_____. *Once More upon a Totem.* Illustrated by Douglas Tait. Atheneum, 1973.

McDermott, Gerald. *Arrow to the Sun: A Pueblo Indian Tale.* Illustrated by Gerald McDermott. Viking, 1974.

Schoolcraft, Henry Rowe. *The Fire Plume: Legends of the American Indians.* Edited by John Bierhorst. Illustrated by Alan E. Cober. Dial, 1969.

_____. *The Ring in the Prairie: A Shawnee Legend.* Edited by John Bierhorst. Illustrated by Leo Dillon and Diane Dillon. Dial, 1970.

Sleator, William. *The Angry Moon.* Illustrated by Blair Lent. Little, Brown, 1970.

Julius Lester

From *Bookpeople: A Multicultural Album* by Sharron L. McElmeel (Libraries Unlimited, Inc., 1992)

Julius Lester

Julius Lester was born on January 27, 1939, in Kansas City, Missouri, and grew up in Kansas and Tennessee. From the beginning of his life he absorbed music and stories from the Southern rural Black tradition—from his father, who was a good storyteller, and from his grandmother, who lived in Arkansas. He began playing the piano at age 5. His favorite things to read were comic books, mysteries, and Westerns.

The first book Lester wrote for children was *To Be a Slave.* He does a lot of research and thinking about his stories before he starts to write them. But once he started to put the words on paper for *To Be a Slave,* he completed it in 3 months. He feels that writing is much more than putting words on paper. He says, "Writing takes place inside me and inside myself, I am always writing." For leisure he browses through scholarly works of history, which often give him ideas for stories.

Stamp collecting is one of his interests. His collection includes stamps from the United States, United Nations, and Israel. He does the *New York Times* crossword puzzle every day and enjoys hiking. His favorite foods are soups and fish. He and his wife, Alida, live in Amherst, Massachusetts, where he has taught at the university since 1971. They are parents to two sons and two daughters: Jody, Malcolm, Elena, and David.

Julius Lester

ABOUT THE AUTHOR

Julius Lester was born January 27, 1939, in Kansas City, Missouri, the son of W. D. and Julia Lester. When Julius was 2, he moved with his family to Kansas City, Kansas; when he was 14, the family settled in Nashville, Tennessee. His father was a Methodist minister who had been brought up in the South. The fact that his father was a great storyteller and had a great love and respect for Black folk culture was a major influence on Julius Lester's life and work. As a young man, Lester often traveled to his maternal grandmother's home in Arkansas. His father's influence, his experiences in Arkansas, and his teenage years in Tennessee shaped his later work.

As a young child, Julius Lester was very interested in music and began playing the piano at the age of 5. For a time he wanted to be a classical pianist, he remembers having a bust of Beethoven on his piano. Lester's story "Basketball Game," which is one of the stories in *Two Love Stories* (Dial, 1972), tells about his growing-up years. He read books of history, mystery stories, and comic books—lots of comic books. He was interested in art, music, and writing, but he always knew he would be a writer. Beginning with books and stories for adults, he entered the field of writing for children and young adults when his adult book editor at Dial suggested that he use his clear and simple writing style to write books for a younger reader. She introduced Lester to Phyllis Fogelman, and they seemed to "hit it off." In discussing his current research on slavery, he told her that he wanted to communicate what it was like to be a slave by telling the story of slavery in the words of slaves. She asked Lester to write a one-page description. He did, she liked it, and he wrote the book in 3 months. *To Be a Slave*, published in 1968, was his first book for a younger audience. Since then he has written more stories about the slave experience and some autobiographical stories; he has also retold many folktales.

Most of Lester's stories for children are based in the South. He uses such interesting sources as early issues of *The Anglo-American Magazine* and volumes of *Judicial Cases* to find ideas and skeletons for his stories. During a personal interview in March 1991, he explained that when he reads something, "Something grows inside. Where that comes from, I don't know that I know. But there is something inside that tells me what needs to be written." Lester continued "I am never not writing. Writing is more than the physical act of putting words on paper. That is the last stage of writing. First and foremost, writing takes place inside me and inside myself, I am always writing."

Lester has written the third volume of his own autobiography. It deals with his struggles to understand himself and the world around him. In the mid-1960s, he joined a student nonviolent group and traveled to North Vietnam to photograph the effects of the U.S. bombing there. He later went to Cuba with Stokely Carmichael. As he wrote and spoke about some of his experiences, some labeled him a black militant—a label he was uncomfortable with. He was a civil rights activist, and many of his photographs of that period are on permanent exhibit in a photographic collection at Howard University. For 8 years he hosted a radio talk show and for 2 years he was host of a PBS live television program. During that time he also recorded two albums of original songs.

In more recent years, Lester has begun to examine his own spirituality. He grew up in a Methodist home but later began to explore many different religions, including Catholicism. Eventually, in 1982, he embraced the Jewish faith and now speaks often on Black-Jewish relations. He also speaks throughout this country and in Europe on topics as diverse as African-American slavery, children's literature, and Black folk literature.

In 1962 Lester married Joan Steinau. Jody, their daughter, was born in 1965 and Malcolm, their son, in 1967. The Lesters divorced in 1970, and 9 years later Julius Lester married Alida Fechner. She had a 7-year-old daughter, Elena, and in 1980 David Julius was born. Since 1971, Lester has taught history, literature, and Judaic studies at the University of Massachusetts. In characterizing his life he says, "My life is very full. I teach, I write, I do a lot of traveling and lecturing. The older I get there seems to be more things that I want to do. My life is really quite wonderful."

THE BOOKSHELF

Lester, Julius. **How Many Spots Does a Leopard Have? And Other Tales.** Illustrated by David Shannon. Scholastic, 1989.

This is a collection of ten African and two Jewish folktales. The stories range from a pourquoi tale to a quest tale of a man trying to win the hand of a beautiful princess. Each tale is illustrated with a full-page oil painting and smaller black-and-white sketches. Warm earth tones are used for the African folktales and a darker palette for the Jewish tales. Source notes are appended.

1. Compare and contrast Lester's version of "Why the Sun and the Moon Live in the Sky" with the picture-book edition, *Why the Sun and the Moon Live in the Sky* by Elphinstone Dayrell, illustrated by Blair Lent (Houghton, 1968, reissued 1991).

2. Compare the illustrations for the African tales to the illustrations for the Jewish tales. Is there a difference? Explain why you think the illustrator would make a distinction.

3. Use the source notes and information within each story to establish the setting of the story. Use clues in the story, such as animals, to identify the geographical setting. Locate the various settings on a map of the world. How does each setting differ from your own setting?

Lester, Julius. **The Knee-High Man and Other Tales.** Illustrated by Ralph Pinto. Dial, 1972.

Talking-beasts tales were brought to this country from Africa. As they were retold in this country, many took on added meanings—meanings associated with the relations between slave and slave owner. Many of the talking-beast tales were collected in *American Negro Folktales* (Fawcett, 1976) by Richard Dorson. He classified them under "Animal and Bird." Lester recalls six of these tales in *The Knee-High Man and Other Tales.* Mr. Rabbit gets the best of Mr. Bear in one story, and a second story, "The Farmer and the Snake," is a realistic one. A farmer helps a poor frozen snake and is bitten in return.

1. Read these tales and discuss the layers of meaning they might have had—both the obvious and the not so obvious, specifically regarding the relationship between slave and slave owner.

2. Categorize the tales into animal and bird stories.

3. Compare and contrast the characters in the tales. Use a character web to help build the comparison (see appendix A).

Lester, Julius. **The Tales of Uncle Remus: The Adventures of Brer Rabbit.** Dial, 1987. **More Tales of Uncle Remus: Further Adventures of Brer Rabbit.** Dial, 1988. **Further Tales of Uncle Remus: The Misadventures of Brer Rabbit, Brer Fox, Brer Wolf, the Doodang, and Other Creatures.** Dial, 1990. All illustrated by Jerry Pinkney.

Lester tells traditional tales that originated in the southern United States and that were retold in Joel Chandler Harris's "Uncle Remus" in the late nineteenth century. Many of the stories include Brer Rabbit, who survives by using his cunning and cleverness against stronger enemies.

1. Compare Uncle Remus's tales with the four tales retold by Priscilla Jaquith in *Bo Rabbit Smart for True: Folktales from the Gullah*, illustrated by Ed Young (Philomel, 1981). These tales were collected from Black people living on the Sea Islands off the coasts of Georgia and South Carolina. The Jaquith tales and the Uncle Remus stories have several motifs in common. Several of them deal with a serious moral often contained in African-American folklore: "Those who look for trouble might find it." African words appear in these stories, such as cooter for tortoise and bittles for victuals. And in the African tradition, the storytellers often repeat words to increase their significance. Onomatopoetia and alliteration add to the poetic quality of the storytelling.

2. In Harris's original version of the Uncle Remus tales, the stories are very difficult to read because of the use of dialect and colloquial language. Compare Julius Lester's versions of the Uncle Remus tales with the versions in some of the following collections and books. Discuss your preferences.

Uncle Remus Retold

Brown, Margaret Wise. *Brer Rabbit: Stories from Uncle Remus.* Illustrated by A. B. Frost. Harper, 1941.

Harris, Joel Chandler. *Brer Rabbit and the Wonderful Tar Baby.* Adapted by Eric Metaxas. Illustrated by Henrik Drescher. Picture Book, 1990.

_____. *Jump! Adventure of Brer Rabbit.* Retold by Van Dyke Parks. Illustrated by Barry Moser. Harcourt, 1986.

_____. *Jump Again! More Adventures of Brer Rabbit.* Retold by Van Dyke Parks. Illustrated by Barry Moser. Harcourt, 1987.

_____. *Jump on Over! The Adventures of Brer Rabbit and His Family.* Retold by Van Dyke Parks. Illustrated by Barry Moser. Harcourt, 1989.

Rees, Ennis. *Brer Rabbit and His Tricks.* Illustrated by Edward Gorey. Young Scott, 1967.

Lester, Julius. **This Strange New Feeling.** Dial, 1982; Scholastic, 1982.

Three stories make up this moving book about slavery and the quest for freedom. When Lester decided he wanted to write three love stories that were set in the horror of slavery, he read through a number of history books until he found the characters he wanted to recreate and bring to life. All three stories are based on actual historical events. The first two are vignettes, one of which tells the story of Ras, who escapes, is recaptured, and attempts to escape once again. The second vignette tells of the slave Maria, wife of the free Black Forrest, who earns enough money to buy her away from her slave owner. When Forrest is accidentally killed, his creditors come to collect his goods. Since Forrest's assets do not cover his debts, and since Maria was never officially freed by her husband, the creditors sell Maria as a slave. The third story is of William and Ellen Craft's flight to the North and freedom. Ellen poses as a white gentleman traveling with "his" personal slave (William). Eventually they must flee again, this time from slave hunters who have come from the South to track down fugitive slaves.

"This Strange New Feeling"

1. Write the next chapter in the life of Ras and Sally. Were they able to keep their freedom or not?

"Where the Sun Lives"

2. After Maria is taken back into slavery, what happens? Who buys her? Does she ever gain her freedom? Does the sun ever shine where she lives?

"A Christmas Love Story"

3. If William or Ellen had kept a journal during their escape to the North, what might they have written? Write two to five sample entries.

4. Pretend you are a slave owner. Defend your right to own slaves.

5. Pretend you are an abolitionist. Write a 2-minute speech supporting legislation repealing the right to own slaves.

6. Locate information about Harriet Tubman. Make a bioposter about her life and her efforts to get other Blacks to freedom. A bioposter is a collage of pictures and information blocks that give information about the subject of the biography.

7. Read one or more of Mildred Taylor's fiction books: *Roll of Thunder, Hear My Cry* (Dial, 1976), or *Let the Circle Be Unbroken* (Dial, 1981). Discuss how life has changed (or not changed) for African Americans from the time of Lester's book (pre-Civil War/1850s) to the 1930s, the setting of Taylor's books.

8. Research the underground railroad and its significance for slaves.

9. Research and write a short paper about the fugitive slave act that Millard Fillmore signed. What significance did it have in "A Christmas Love Story?"

Lester, Julius. **To Be a Slave.** Illustrated by Tom Feelings. Dial, 1968; Scholastic, 1968.

Through the words of slaves Lester tells of the humiliation and ostracism of slavery. The vivid, painful descriptions and narrative combine verbatim testimony of former slaves with the author's own commentary. The publisher suggests this title for readers age 14 and up; a read-aloud audience may be younger.

1. Correlate the activities for this book with those suggested for *This Strange New Feeling* (see preceding entry).

2. Use documents and journals to establish background for understanding the institution of slavery. Milton Meltzer has compiled three volumes that provide reproductions of primary sources, including letters, speeches, excerpts from books, and court testimony: *In Their Own Words: A History of the American Negro, 1619-1865* (Crowell, 1964); *In Their Own Words: A History of the American Negro, 1865-1916* (Crowell, 1965); and *In Their Own Words: A History of the American Negro, 1916-1966* (Crowell, 1967). In 1984 these three volumes were revised, updated, and published in a single volume, *Black Americans: A History in Their Own Words* (Crowell, 1964, 1984).

FURTHER READING

When Lester's book *To Be a Slave* was named a Newbery honor book in 1968, Lester became the first African American to achieve that honor. The first African American to receive the Newbery Award (1975) was Virginia Hamilton for *M. C. Higgins the Great* (Macmillan, 1974). She has written more than forty novels about African Americans in a contemporary setting. Hamilton has also collected many African-American stories into a collection titled *The People Could Fly* (Knopf, 1985), illustrated by Leo Dillon and Diane Dillon. *The People Could Fly* is divided into four sections:

*   "He Lion, Bruh Bear, and Bruh Rabbit and Other Animal Tales"

*   "The Beautiful Girl of the Moon Tower and Other Tales of the Real, Extravagant, and Fanciful"

*   "John and the Devil's Daughter and Other Tales of the Supernatural"

*   "Carrying the Running-Aways and Other Slave Tales of Freedom"

"Carrying the Running-Aways" in the last section is a narrative that tells the story of a slave who rowed runaways across the Ohio River to freedom. On the Ohio River side, John Rankin, an abolitionist, helped start the slaves to freedom through the underground railroad system. One of those John Rankin helped was Hamilton's own grandfather, Levi Perry, who crossed the Ohio River with his mother about 1854. Levi Perry had ten children, one of whom was Hamilton's mother, Etta Belle Perry Hamilton. Hamilton's stories should not be missed. (Author Virginia Hamilton's life is profiled in a filmstrip/cassette presentation from American School Publishers, *Meet the Newbery Author: Virginia Hamilton.*)

Patricia McKissack

From *Bookpeople: A Multicultural Album* by Sharron L. McElmeel (Libraries Unlimited, Inc., 1992)

Patricia McKissack

Patricia L'Ann Carwell McKissack, the daughter of Robert and Erma Carwell, was born August 9, 1944, in Nashville, Tennessee. Her growing-up years were spent in the South. She remembers fondly the hot summer nights when her mother read poetry by Paul Dunbar, especially "Little Brown Baby"—her favorite. Later when Patricia McKissack began to write, her first published book was *Paul Laurence Dunbar: A Poet to Remember*. She quickly became known for her biographies of important people such as Martin Luther King, Jr., Mary McLeod Bethune, and A. Philip Randolf, who led the struggle to unionize Pullman porters.

Other stories come from Patricia McKissack's own family. After she saw a picture of her grandparents winning a cakewalk, she wrote the story *Mirandy and Brother Wind*. Mirandy is named after her husband's grandmother, Miranda. And Mrs. Poinsettia in the story is much like a woman Patricia McKissack knew in Mississippi. Jerry Pinkney drew Mrs. Poinsettia to look like his wife, Gloria. A book Patricia McKissack wrote about twins, *Who Is Who?*, features her twin sons Robert and John as Bobby and Johnny.

At one time Patricia McKissack taught junior high English, but now she and her husband, Frederick, own a writing service. They live in a large remodeled inner-city home in St. Louis, Missouri, where Patricia McKissack enjoys gardening and growing roses. They have three grown sons—Frederick, Jr., Robert Lewis, and John Patrick.

Patricia McKissack

ABOUT THE AUTHOR

Patricia L'Ann Carwell McKissack describes herself as a wordsmith, that is, someone who uses words to build images. She also uses words to teach children of all races about many aspects of African-American culture.

Patricia McKissack was born August 9, 1944, in Nashville, Tennessee, to Robert and Erma Carwell, who were both civil servants. McKissack grew up reading and listening. She listened to her mother read poems on hot summer nights and listened to stories her grandparents told; later she would use these experiences to create books for other young children to read.

McKissack attended Tennessee State University and earned a B.A. degree in 1964. On December 12, 1965, she married Frederick L. McKissack. By 1975 the McKissacks had three children (Frederick, Jr., and twins Robert and John), and Patricia McKissack had earned a master's degree from Webster University. For a while McKissack taught junior high school English and wrote when she had the time. Soon she put teaching aside and became a children's book editor. During this period her first book, *Paul Laurence Dunbar: A Poet to Remember*, was published. Within the next few years, she wrote several biographies of important African Americans and became noted for the candor and depth with which she treated her topics. In her nonfiction work, she often included controversial topics such as racism but was cited as being evenhanded in her writing and presentation of any issue. Patricia McKissack and Frederick McKissack have collaborated on a book for young adults that examines the problem of racism, *Taking a Stand against Racism and Racial Discrimination* (Watts, 1990). They also coauthored a biography, *W. E. B. Du Bois* (Watts, 1990). It is a scholarly work that examines Du Bois's background and his life's work to lift up his people.

McKissack also became known for her fiction. Especially well received were her nostalgic picture books, set in the rural South, that blend reality with a touch of fantasy. Her young Black female protagonists are assertive and know how to take care of themselves. She adapted several traditional stories into condensed versions for beginning readers. Those in general are not as successful as her other writing endeavors, with the exception of *Monkey-Monkey's Trick: Based on an African Folk Tale*. That story seems to be particularly suited to emerging readers. The repetitive trickster tale appeals to both listeners and readers. Her easy-to-ready titles that are original stories, such as *Who Is Who?* and *Messy Bessey*, have also been successful.

As a wordsmith, McKissack likes the sounds of words and maneuvers them to say what she wants them to say. She uses her word skills to tells stories about African-American people. McKissack feels that it is the specific stories of great people that spice up basic facts and general information. One person McKissack tells stories about is Mary McLeod Bethune, who started a school with just a few dollars. That school, Bethune Cookman College, is still operating in Daytona Beach, Florida. Bethune loved to speak to children. From the day she began to teach, she spoke of a world as beautiful as a flower garden, in which people were like flowers, all blooming differently, at different times. One young boy observed that there were no black flowers. Later, Bethune went through Holland, where they presented her with the first black tulips. She used that as confirmation of her belief that "because you have not seen a thing does not mean it does not exist." Bethune is also called "the Black Rose" because a rose was developed in her honor.

McKissack believes that we must learn to share moments—including moments and stories from history. We must tell those stories in such a way that children will want to hear and read more stories. Another story she tells is of Elijah McCoy, a story about the origin of the phrase "I want the real McCoy." That phrase came about at the turn of the century when there were no mandatory school laws and children worked in factories. Often, 6- or 7-year-olds would be used to climb over machinery to oil or grease it. That practice originated the term "grease monkey." Children often got hurt, but mechanics did not shut down the machines. Elijah McCoy, an orphan, slept under the machinery. It was a warm place to sleep, but he also watched and learned how the machinery worked. He developed a mechanism that self-oiled the machines, but the patent office refused to patent the self-oiler because Elijah McCoy was Black. So his idea was open for others to take, which many did, developing their own adaptations. However, the mechanisms made by others did not work very well, so people began asking for the "real McCoy."

McKissack does not like people putting age levels on her books, many of which have varied uses. For example, one of her easy-to-read Rookie Reader® books, *Who Is Coming?*, has been used with high school students. It is a guessing game of sorts, a game that takes place in Africa. McKissack starts by asking students if Africa is a continent or a country. If they know it's a continent composed of many countries, how many know the names of more than two of those countries? Most will know Ethiopia (where people are starving) and South Africa (where people are oppressed). And, if Africa is a continent, are people who live in Egypt African, just as people who live in Italy or France are European? What else do students know about Africa? Many picture it as one big jungle filled with animals. In fact, only 20 percent of Africa is jungle. A third of the continent is covered by the Sahara Desert. There are savannah lands and, of course, jungle. So when *Who Is Coming?* is read, the first clues point to a reptile—either an alligator or a crocodile. Since alligators do not live in Africa, it must be a crocodile. Other African animals that are highlighted are the snake, leopard, lion, elephant, and hippopotamus. Could the last animal featured in the book be a tiger? And "why didn't little monkey run from the tiger"? Because there are no tigers in Africa—tigers are Asiatic animals. This book is not as simple as it would seem on the surface.

McKissack's stories often instruct while conveying a pride in African-American heritage. One story inspired from the author's own family involves the cakewalk, a dance. One day McKissack came across a photograph of her grandparents winning a cakewalk, a dance rooted in African-American culture. Her grandfather boasted that his wife's dancing had captured the wind. The story that developed became *Mirandy and Brother Wind*. McKissack's husband's grandmother's name was Miranda, but that name jolted the flow of the language—it was too harsh. So she changed Miranda to Mirandy. The book also posed some illustration problems. For example, Jerry Pinkney had to devise a way to illustrate Brother Wind. As a child McKissack had been associated with the African Methodist Episcopal Church in Mississippi. At that church she remembered a woman who by wearing red on Sunday scandalized the more conservative townspeople. Ms. Poinsettia is a lot like that woman. When Pinkney began to create an image for her, he drew a picture of a woman who looked a lot like his own wife, Gloria. The illustrations earned a Caldecott honor award.

Pinkney's illustrations are very authentic, but McKissack has praise for her other illustrators as well. In a presentation in Atlanta, Georgia, on May 9, 1990, McKissack spoke about Scott Cook and said, "He is white but was able to develop a love and a feel for the work of an African American." He created the illustrations for *Nettie Jo's Friends*. McKissack says that he was knowledgeable about customs and even realized that the phrase "piney woods" is a southern phrase that indicates a stand of trees, not necessarily a woods filled with pine trees. Rachel Isodora is a New Yorker whose grandfather told her stories in Yiddish, so her illustrations for *Flossie and the Fox* reflect the skill of the storyteller. Each of McKissack's books has, in its own way, contributed to the building of bridges between cultures. *Flossie and the Fox* has been translated into French, German, Swedish, and Afrikaans.

Patricia and Frederick McKissack live in St. Louis, Missouri, where they own All-Writing Services, a business that caters to the writing needs of a wide variety of clients. They write business brochures, instruction manuals, and books. Their sons, Frederick, Jr., Robert, and John, are beginning their own lives. And Patricia McKissack continues to bring her heritage to readers through her writing. In the Atlanta presentation she said that she "is not a black writer but rather a writer who happens to be black—I write for children of all races."

THE BOOKSHELF

McKissack, Patricia. **Flossie and the Fox.** Illustrated by Rachel Isadora. Dial, 1986.

In a satisfying reversal tale of "Red Riding Hood," Flossie shows that she has what it takes to outwit the fox. Flossie Findley's mission is to carry eggs through the Tennessee forest to Miz Viola. She must watch out for the "ol' slickster" fox, who loves eggs. Isadora created her illustrations, realistic figures and impressionistic backgrounds, with watercolor and ink.

1. Before reading this story, compare with students versions of the traditional "Little Red Riding Hood" story. Brief comparison notes follow the booklist.

"Little Red Riding Hood" — A Traditional Tale

deRegniers, Beatrice Schenk. *Red Riding Hood: Retold in Verse for Boys and Girls to Read Themselves.* Illustrated by Edward Gorey. Atheneum, 1972. (Filmstrip/cassette format is available from Weston Woods®.)

Hogrogian, Nonny, illustrator. *The Renowned History of Little Red Riding Hood.* Crowell, 1967.

Hyman, Trina Schart. *Little Red Riding Hood.* Holiday, 1983. (1984 Caldecott honor book)

Marshall, James. *Red Riding Hood.* Dial, 1987

Perrault, Charles. *The Little Red Riding Hood.* Illustrated by William Stobbs. Walck, 1972.

Rockwell, Anne. "Little Red Riding Hood." In *The Three Bears & 15 Other Stories.* Illustrated by Anne Rockwell. Crowell, 1975; Harper Trophy, 1984.

Zwerger, Lisbeth. *Little Red Cap.* Retold and illustrated by Lisbeth Zwerger. Morrow, 1983.

Comparison Notes — "Little Red Riding Hood"

This tale has been retold by many storytellers and illustrated by as many artists. Some of the illustrations clearly depict the setting (Hyman's is the Black Forest of Germany), while others are less distinctive. Little Red Riding Hood herself is both droll (as in the illustrations by Gorey for the deRegniers version), and beautiful (Hyman version), and the wolf is both friendly and menacing. The story grammar is quite similar, even though details vary. Baskets are filled with slightly different food items. Red Riding Hood usually picks small flowers, as normally found on the grassy floor of a dense woods, but Marshall's version adds a touch of Texas when he has his Red Riding Hood pick giant sunflowers.

Hyman puts a guardian cat in almost every frame of her retelling; and Hyman herself, as a child, is Little Red Riding Hood. The versions collected from the Grimm Brothers tradition usually have a more violent ending than those versions that cite Charles Perrault as their source. Full comparison notes for the "Red Riding Hood" tale and response suggestions are included in the entry for deRegniers's *Red Riding Hood*, in *An Author a Month (for Pennies)* by Sharron McElmeel (Libraries Unlimited, 1988), pages 102-104.

2. Compare *Flossie and the Fox* and "Little Red Riding Hood" with Virginia Hamilton's "A Wolf and Little Daughter" in *The People Could Fly: American Black Folktales*, illustrated by Leo Dillon and Diane Dillon (Knopf, 1985), pages 60-63. (A. Delaney's *The Gunnywolf* [Harper, 1988] has many of the same story elements as "A Wolf and Little Daughter.")

3. Adults who wish to become more familiar with the variations of "Little Red Riding Hood" will find useful a collection of tales, *Little Red Riding Hood* (Green Tiger, 1989), compiled by Edens Cooper. Illustrations by Arthur Rackham, Charles Robinson, Jessie Willcox Smith, and others are featured.

4. Extend students' appreciation of this book by setting up a listening/viewing center with a filmstrip/cassette version. *Flossie and the Fox* in filmstrip/cassette form is available from Weston Woods®. A read-along cassette is also available.

McKissack, Patricia, and Frederick McKissack. **A Long Hard Journey: The Story of the Pullman Porter.** Walker, 1989.

After the Civil War, George Pullman offered the newly freed slaves steady jobs in his luxurious Pullman cars. But the status-filled jobs were soon exposed for their long hours, low pay, and threat of lost jobs for the meanest of reasons, including any response porters might have given to harrassment by racist passengers. In 1894 Eugene Debs attempted unsuccessfully to unionize the railroad, but he excluded Blacks. It was left to A. Philip Randolph to pursue the organization of Black porters. After a long struggle, he gained success when the Brotherhood of Sleeping Car Porters was organized in 1925. The organization's first contract with a corporation was signed in 1937.

1. Introduce to students A. Philip Randolph and his unionizing work.

About A. Philip Randolph

Asa Philip Randolph was born in Crescent City, Florida, but moved to New York City as a young man. He held odd jobs during the day and attended City College of New York at night. A socialist at the time of World War I, he later became convinced that unions offered African Americans the best chance for a fair wage. A group of Pullman car porters requested that he organize and lead a union for them. The union was established in 1925 and signed its first corporate contract in 1937. In 1941 Randolph threatened to march on Washington, D.C., to demand jobs for African Americans in defense industries. That threat was instrumental in President Franklin D. Roosevelt's decision to establish the Fair Employment Practices Committee. In 1963 Randolph helped organize a Washington march to protest injustice to African Americans.

2. It might be difficult to interest young readers in this topic. However, reading aloud excerpts can pique interest in the entire work or in related topics. Poetry and railroad songs are used as chapter headings. Black-and-white historical photographs illustrate the book. Share excerpts, the poetry, and the historical photographs to build interest.

3. Pullman cars were named after George Pullman. Words that originate from someone's name are known as eponyms. Study other eponyms and the people on whose names the words are based. A reference source, *The Eponyms Dictionaries Index*, edited by James A. Ruffner (Gale, 1977), will help identify words that are "people words." Locate the origin of graham cracker, ferris wheel, poinsettia, and other eponyms. William and Mary Morris have written several reference books that deal with word and phrase origin, including eponyms. Don't miss *Guppies in Tuxedos: Funny Eponyms* by Marvin Terban (Clarion 1988). Other word and phrase origins can be located by using the subject heading ENGLISH LANGUAGE—ETYMOLOGY.

McKissack, Patricia. **Martin Luther King, Jr.: A Man to Remember.** Children's, 1984.

McKissack covers King's relationship with other Black leaders, movements, politicians, and the FBI. Poems from various Black authors at the beginning of each chapter set the tone for what follows. A timeline at the end of the book helps readers see what was going on in other parts of the world during that period. McKissack gives background information to help readers for whom King is a historical figure know why he was important to the development of the civil rights movement. This book does not avoid the subject of racism.

1. Introduce Martin Luther King, Jr., and his role in the struggle for civil rights.

About Martin Luther King, Jr.

In January 1986 the United States observed the first official holiday honoring Martin Luther King, Jr. King was born January 15, 1929, but the celebration of his birthday is officially designated as the third Monday in January. King was a civil rights leader who dreamed that someday people of all races and religions would find a way to live together peacefully.

2. Share a poem about Martin Luther King, Jr. Two you may want to use are "Dreams" by Langston Hughes in *The Dreamkeeper and Other Poems* by Langston Hughes (Knopf, 1932; 1960) and "Martin Luther King Day" by Myra Cohn Livingston in *Celebrations* (Holiday, 1985).

3. Share an excerpt from the August 28, 1963, "I Have a Dream" speech, which Martin Luther King, Jr., gave in Washington, D.C. Discuss your dreams.

I Have a Dream

I have a dream today.
I have a dream that one day every valley shall be exalted ... So let freedom ring ... From every mountainside, let freedom ring. And when we allow freedom to ring, when we let it ring from every village, from every hamlet, from every state and every city, we will be able to speed up the day when all of God's children ... will be able to join hands and sing ... "Free at last. Free at last! Thank God almighty, we are free at last!"
—Martin Luther King, Jr.

4. Introduce students to other books about Martin Luther King, Jr.

Martin Luther King, Jr.

Adler, David A. *A Picture Book of Martin Luther King, Jr.* Illustrated by Robert Casilla. Holiday, 1989; Scholastic, 1989. (A filmstrip/cassette and a video based on this book are available from Live Oak Media.)

Darby, Jean. *Martin Luther King, Jr.* Lerner, 1990.

de Kay, James T. *Meet Martin Luther King, Jr.* Illustrated with photographs. Random House, 1969 (1989). (Step-Up Biographies)

Haskins, James. *The Life and Death of Martin Luther King, Jr.* Lothrop, 1977.

Patrick, Diane. *Martin Luther King, Jr.* Watts, 1990. (First Book Series)

Rowland, Della. *Martin Luther King, Jr.: The Dream of Peaceful Revolution.* Burdett, 1990. (History of Civil Rights Movement Series)

Smith, Kathie Billingslea. *Martin Luther King, Jr.* Illustrated by James Seward. Julian Messner, 1987. (The Great Americans Series)

5. Martin Luther King, Jr., was influenced by the teaching of Mohandas Gandhi. Investigate Gandhi's beliefs and life. Discuss with students how his views on life might have influenced King.

6. Make a bioposter depicting some important events in King's life.

7. Reverend Ralph David Abernathy was very involved in the struggle for civil rights with Dr. King. Have students locate some information about Abernathy and write a short informational paper about him.

8. Lead a class discussion on the issue of civil rights and have students write letters to the president of the United States sharing some of their ideas about the status of equal rights in America and suggesting changes that might be made.

9. When Martin Luther King, Jr., was in the seventh and eighth grades, he went to a special school. He learned about Harriet Tubman, Frederick Douglass, Denmark Vesey, and Nat Turner. Have the class investigate these people.

10. Have students make a list of ten interesting facts they have found about Martin Luther King, Jr.

11. Dr. King was awarded the Nobel Peace Prize. Have the class research the significance and history of that award, the reasons King received it, and names of other people who have been so honored.

McKissack, Patricia. **Mary McLeod Bethune: A Great American Educator.** Children's 1985.

Mary McLeod Bethune was a great educator, Black leader, and adviser to many, including President Franklin D. Roosevelt. As the first free-born child of her freed slave parents, she taught hundreds of African-American children to read. Bethune had to struggle for her own education. She basically educated herself and went on to build a school, which is still in operation today as Bethune Cookman College.

1. Introduce Mary McLeod Bethune and her work in educating others.

About Mary McLeod Bethune

Mary McLeod Bethune (pronounced buh-THOON) was born in 1875 in Mayesville, South Carolina, into a southern sharecropper's family. She was the fifteenth child, and the first born free, of seventeen children. She attended a mission school, a seminary, and the Moody Bible Institute. But her education was a struggle, and she was in many ways self-educated. In 1904, at the age of 29, she opened a school for "Negro children" at Daytona Beach, Florida. She fought the Ku Klux Klan, segregation, and race riots. She helped establish mission schools for African-American children. Later, in 1923, the Florida school merged with a college and survives as Bethune Cookman College. In 1935 Mary McLeod Bethune was awarded the Spingarn Medal. She served as president of Bethune Cookman College until 1942, when she entered government service. She became an adviser to departments and people in the government, including President Franklin D. Roosevelt. Her work in the government helped to open the doors of government to African Americans. In 1954 she was named "Mother of the Century" by the Dorie Miller Foundation. Mary McLeod Bethune died in 1955.

2. Introduce students to other books about Mary McLeod Bethune.

Mary McLeod Bethune

Greenfield, Eloise. *Mary McLeod Bethune.* Illustrated by Jerry Pinkney. Crowell, 1977.

Meltzer, Milton. *Mary McLeod Bethune: Voice of Black Hope.* Illustrated by Stephen Marchesi. Viking, 1987; Puffin, 1988.

3. Mary McLeod Bethune was born in 1875 and died in 1955. Help students make a timeline of significant events that occurred in American history during her lifetime. A computer program that could be used to help students construct the timeline is *Timeliner* from Tom Snyder Productions.

McKissack, Patricia, and Frederick McKissack. **Messy Bessey.** Illustrations by Richard Hackney. Children's, 1987. (Rookie Reader®)

This gentle story about a little girl dealing with an everyday situation is for emerging readers. Bessey's room is quite messy, but she sets out to clean it. She stuffs things into her closet until her room is clean and beautiful (just like Bessey).

1. When Bessey cleans her room, she stuffs almost everything into her closet until the room looks very clean. Have students draw a picture of their own closet after their room is cleaned.

2. Bessey has a sign over her door, "Bessey's Place." Set up a sign-making station in the classroom. At the station include fat and thin markers, pencils, crayons, cardboard, and colored oak tag or railroad board. Encourage students to make a sign for their bedroom door.

McKissack, Patricia. **Mirandy and Brother Wind.** Illustrated by Jerry Pinkney. Knopf, 1988.

Mirandy is determined to catch Brother Wind and have him for her partner in the upcoming junior cakewalk. She tries various "folk wisdom" tactics and eventually succeeds in trapping her prey in the barn. At first she plans to "make Brother Wind do her bidding" and be her partner at the cakewalk. But she ends up dancing with Ezel, and, with the help of Brother Wind, they dance with the wind.

1. In the story Mirandy visits a conjure woman to get advice about methods to use to catch Brother Wind. Precede the reading of McKissack's story by reading *The Ballad of Belle Dorcus* by William H. Hooks, illustrated by Brian Pinkney (Knopf, 1990), a tale that introduces the conjure woman as a character in southern folklore. An author's note at the beginning of Hooks's tale explains the existence of conjure women in southern legends. See the index for reference to Hooks's title. What advice would you seek?

2. Use watercolors or a favorite art medium to create a suitable cake to be given as a prize in the cakewalk.

3. Read some poems about the wind. Don't miss "Who Has Seen the Wind?" by Christina Rossetti. One source is *The Random House Book of Poetry*, a collection of poems selected by Jack Prelutsky and illustrated by Arnold Lobel (Random, 1983). That source also contains several other poems about the wind.

4. Compare the illustrations created by Jerry Pinkney for McKissack's book with those created by Pinkney for Robert D. San Souci's *The Talking Eggs: A Folktale from the American South* (Dial, 1989). The illustrations for both books were created with watercolors. Readers will recognize in both stories the hens, the setting, the young girl's clothing, etc. A videotape of *The Talking Eggs* is available from American School Publishers.

McKissack, Patricia. **Monkey-Monkey's Trick: Based on an African Folk Tale.** Illustrated by Paul Meisel. Random, 1988. (A Step into Reading Book: Step 2)

Monkey-Monkey asks for help in building his house, but Elephant, Giraffe, and Lion all have something else to do. So Monkey-Monkey begins the task by himself. Hyena offers to help, but Monkey-Monkey doesn't trust him. Hyena comes back to trick Monkey-Monkey, but Monkey-Monkey has a trick of his own.

1. The beginning of the story brings in elements of "Little Red Hen" and of a trickster. Compare the story to "Little Red Hen" and to Keiko Kasza's tale of trickery, *The Wolf's Chicken Stew* (Putnam, 1987).

2. When Hyena figures out what has happened, what do you think he will do? Is there a sequel story you could write about the next time Hyena tries to trick Monkey-Monkey?

3. Read other folk stories that feature a monkey. Use a character web (see Appendix A) to help compare/contrast the portrayal of the monkey in folktales. In the Congo the monkey appears occasionally as the opponent of the trickster. In the "Americas" the monkey is almost absent as a character except occasionally in tales told in Brazil and a few other South American countries.

Monkeys in Folklore

Galdone, Paul. *The Monkey and the Crocodile: A Jataka Tale from India*. Illustrated by Paul Galdone. Clarion, 1969.

Guy, Rosa. *Mother Crocodile*. Illustrated by John Steptoe. Delacorte, 1981.

Kepes, Juliet. *Five Little Monkeys*. Illustrated by Juliet Kepes. Houghton, 1952.

Wolkstein, Diane. *The Cool Ride in the Sky*. Illustrated by Paul Galdone. Knopf, 1973.

McKissack, Patricia. **Nettie Jo's Friends.** Illustrated by Scott Cook. Knopf, 1989.

Nettie Jo's mother is sewing Nettie Jo a new dress for a wedding. But Nettie Jo wants her doll, Annie Mae, to have a new dress, too. She has the cloth, but all the sewing needles seem to be in use by the women who are preparing for the wedding. So Nettie Jo sets out to find her own needle. She asks the help of a rabbit, a fox, and, finally, a panther.

1. Compare Nettie Jo, Flossie (from *Flossie and the Fox*), and Mirandy (from *Mirandy and Brother Wind*). What characteristics do they have in common?

2. Discuss whether you would like Nettie Jo for a friend. Why or why not?

3. Design a dress for Nettie Jo to wear to the wedding.

4. Scott Cook also illustrated *The Gingerbread Boy* (Knopf, 1989). Compare his illustrations in that title to those in *Nettie Jo's Friends*. Did he use a similar technique? Do they invoke a similar image, that is, sunny or dull, happy or sad, etc?

McKissack, Patricia, and Frederick McKissack. **Who Is Who?** Illustrated by Elizabeth M. Allen. Children's, 1983. (A Rookie Reader®)

This is a delightful story of twins Bobby and Johnny. A page showing Bobby dressing himself all in blue, with the caption "Bobby likes blue," is preceded by a similar image of Johnny dressing in red, with the caption "Johnny likes red." Following is a page showing both of them together (one in red, the other in blue), with the caption "Who is who?" The book continues with additional illustrations for hot and cold, front and back, up and down, big and little, and over and under.

1. This is an amusing introduction to the idea of identical twins. Read more about twins in the following books.

Twins and More Twins

Aliki. *Jack and Jake.* Illustrated by Aliki. Greenwillow, 1986.

Hutchins, Pat. *Which Witch Is Which?* Illustrated by Pat Hutchins. Greenwillow, 1989.

McDermott, Gerald. *The Magic Tree: A Tale from the Congo.* Illustrated by Gerald McDermott. Holt, 1973.

Neasi, Barbara J. *Just Like Me.* Illustrated by Lois Axeman. Children's, 1984.

Simon, Norma. *How Do I Feel?* Illustrated by Joe Lasker. Whitman, 1970.

Yorinks, Arthur. *Oh, Brother.* Illustrated by Richard Egielski. Farrar, 1989.

2. Invite twins to visit your class and talk about being twins. Distinguish between identical or fraternal twins. And to learn more about twins and being a twin, read *Being a Twin, Having a Twin* by Maxine B. Rosenberg (Greenwillow, 1985).

3. Distinguishing between identical twins is carried one step further in a book about identical triplets, *My Three Uncles*, by Yossi Abolafia (Greenwillow, 1985). In this book a young girl learns to distinguish between her uncles. Her Uncle Max says, "Just watch us very closely and you'll see how different we are." The story shows very clearly that even identical twins or triplets are really quite different; looks are only skin deep. Make a list of likenesses and differences between parents or between siblings.

FURTHER READING

Patricia McKissack has said, "I am not a black writer, I am a writer who happens to be black – I write for children of all races." Not only do children of African-American heritage need to have access to the stories that McKissack writes, but children of all other races also need to have these stories read to them and shared and savored with them. Set aside a specific time each day to read aloud stories from a variety of cultures, races, and religions. But do not confine your reading to folk literature. Although folk literature is more readily available, it, alone, will not give a balanced view of society today.

Nicholasa Mohr

From *Bookpeople: A Multicultural Album* by Sharron L. McElmeel (Libraries Unlimited, Inc., 1992)

Nicholasa Mohr

Pedro and Nicholasa Golpé came to the United States from Puerto Rico in the 1930s. Their daughter, Nicholasa, was born November 1, 1939, in El Barrio, a section of New York City. The family moved to the Bronx about the time Nicholasa started school. Nicholasa enjoyed drawing and creating her own world. Nicholasa's mother encouraged her art work. She told Nicholasa that she must make an important contribution to the world; she must be somebody. Both of Nicholasa's parents died before she finished school, and she was sent to an aunt's house to live. Her six older brothers went to live in other places.

Nicholasa Mohr wanted to attend art school but ended up attending a trade high school. Eventually she did study art and even went to Mexico to study printmaking. She became a very well-known artist, and her work was exhibited in many galleries. She married Irwin Mohr and they had two sons, David and Jason. The family moved to Teaneck, New Jersey, and she set up an artist's studio in the attic of their house. One of the people who collected her artwork encouraged her to write a story about growing up in El Barrio. *Nilda*, her first novel, was published in 1973. Now she is a full-time writer.

Nicholasa Mohr, now a widow, lives in a townhouse in Brooklyn, New York, with her cat, Winnie. Her sons, David and Jason, are grown. Her favorite things include vegetarian food, yoga, and walking.

Nicholasa Mohr

ABOUT THE AUTHOR/ILLUSTRATOR

Nicholasa Mohr as born November 1, 1939, in El Barrio, a section of New York City also known as Spanish Harlem. El Barrio means "the neighborhood" and this neighborhood was predominantly Puerto Rican. Mohr's parents, Pedro and Nicholasa Golpé, came to the United States from Puerto Rico in the 1930s, during the Great Depression. They brought with them four small sons, and three more children were born in the United States. Nicholasa was the youngest child and the only girl. The family moved to the Bronx about the time Nicholasa started school. She got her first library card when she was 7 years old, and the first book she chose was Collodi's *Pinocchio*. By the time she was 8, her father had died. Her mother worked hard to keep the family together, but when she could no longer work, she had to apply for public assistance. Mohr writes about a similar instance in *Nilda* ("Late November, 1941," pages 62-71). Both of Nicholasa's parents had dreams for their children, and all those dreams included education. After her husband's death, Nicholasa's mother continued to encourage all her children to study, to make something of themselves. Nicholasa loved to paint and draw, and she was able to use her talents to set herself apart from the other children at school. Although the family continued to struggle economically, Nicholasa's mother continued to encourage her in her art.

Later in her life, Mohr wrote a book, *Felita*, about an incident in her life. Felita's family was hassled and harassed in their new all-white neighborhood and had to move back to their old neighborhood because of fear for their well-being. However, the family not only survived but thrived. Nicholasa's family had a similar setback. Nicholasa said, "We too were beaten, harassed and had to move out of an all-white ethnic neighborhood and return to our old neighborhood." And like Felita's family, Nicholasa's family managed through very difficult times. While Nicholasa was still in junior high school, her mother died in poverty. The family split up and Nicholasa went to live in her aunt's home, where her presence was just tolerated.

Nicholasa was a very talented artist, but instead of recommending a school that would lead to college, her school counselor channeled her to a trade school where she could learn a trade and not be "a burden on society." A poor Hispanic stood little chance of getting a college education, and the counselor's attitude was that Nicholasa should not take the place of someone who was more likely to go to college. So Nicholasa went to the trade school but managed to avoid all the sewing courses. She disliked sewing and still does. She studied fashion illustrating instead and eventually managed to study art. When she finished high school, she enrolled in the Art Students' League in New York City, where she studied painting and drawing. During her high school years she worked in the public library and became acquainted with books that displayed the work of Mexican muralists and artists. She knew that she wanted to go to Mexico to study art, so she saved enough money to spend a semester in Mexico studying printmaking. Seeing the work of the great Mexican muralists helped to shape the direction of her future artwork.

After returning to the United States Mohr enrolled in the New School for Social Research in New York City, where she met her husband-to-be, Brooklyn native Irwin Mohr, who was working on a doctorate in clinical psychology. After a rather short courtship they were married. When they had two sons, they moved to an old wooden house in Teaneck, New Jersey, a suburb of New York City. The house had a huge attic, which Nicholasa converted into an art studio with a printmaking press. She became a successful artist, whose work appeared in many exhibitions and art galleries. In 1972 one of the people who regularly bought her art, an editor at a publishing house, asked if Mohr would consider writing about growing up Puerto Rican. At first she declined, but when she realized how little had been written about Puerto Ricans, she decided to try. She wrote fifty pages of short stories about her life, but after reading the stories the publisher was not interested. She wanted more sensational episodes—gang fights, drug dealing, encounters with the police. But that was not what Nicholasa's life had been about, so she declined to rewrite the manuscript.

In a few weeks, however, Nicholasa got a call from an editor from Harper & Row. The editor was interested in Mohr's artwork, but Mohr asked her to read her manuscript. Three weeks later she had a signed contract, and her first book, *Nilda*, was published in 1973. She also created the eight illustrations for that book and designed the book jacket as well. Vincent, her second oldest brother, encouraged her to start a second book of short stories. *El Bronx Remembered* contained twelve short stories and a novella. She began to concentrate more on her written art and less and less on her visual art. By 1979 *In Nueva York* and *Felita* were published. When her husband died and her sons went off to school, Mohr moved from her house in Teaneck to a narrow townhouse in the Park Slope section of Brooklyn.

Nicholasa Mohr no longer works as a visual artist, except for her own personal enjoyment, but concentrates instead on writing fiction and essays. In 1986 *Going Home*, a sequel to *Felita*, was published. Books by Mohr have garnered the American Book Award and the Jane Addams Children's Book Award and have been listed on several best-book and notable-book lists, including those published by the *School Library Journal* and the American Library Association. In 1991 Random House will publish a literary fairy tale she is writing. She is also in the process of writing a middle-grade novel for Lothrop and a series of chapter books for Random House.

Nicholasa Mohr has conducted many workshops and classes in communities throughout New York and at various universities and colleges. Since 1989 she has been a distinguished visiting professor at Queens College in the Department of Elementary and Early Childhood and Services. In May 1989 she was awarded an honorary degree of Doctor of Letters by the State University of New York. Nicholasa Mohr, a poor Puerto Rican girl from El Barrio, is now Dr. Nicholasa Mohr, successful author and artist.

THE BOOKSHELF

Mohr, Nicholasa. **Felita.** Illustrated by Ray Cruz. Dial, 1979; Bantam, 1990.

Felita feels right at home in her neighborhood. She knows just about everyone: Gigi, Paquito, Consuela, Joanie, Doña Josefina in the bodega, and old Bernie and his cat, Mr. Roosevelt. Felita plays some of her favorite games in the street. But the family moves to a "better neighborhood," and the family's presence is met with prejudice and resentment. Nicholasa Mohr says that some of the incidents she recounts in *Felita* are based on childhood experiences.

1. Read chapter 2 aloud and discuss how new students in your school and your neighborhood are treated. Make a list of actions that could be taken to make a new person feel welcome.

2. Compare your life and neighborhood with Felita's "home" neighborhood. Do you play the same games, do the same things?

3. Discuss the setting of this story and compare it with that of other familiar books, such as Beverly Cleary's Ramona books or Lois Lowry's Anatasia books.

Mohr, Nicholasa. **Going Home.** Dial, 1986; Bantam, 1989.

Felita Maldonado's story from *Felita* continues in this growing-up novel. In this story Felita finds a boyfriend and spends a summer in Puerto Rico.

1. Locate Puerto Rico on a map. Gather information about the country and write a report or make a presentation, a mobile, a diorama of the country, an information chart, or notebook.

2. Read aloud some of the episodes that take place in Puerto Rico and note the parts that give information about the setting.

3. Discuss whether or not you would like to have Felita as a friend. Make a list of Felita's characteristics; then list your own characteristics. Do you and Felita have any common characteristics?

Mohr, Nicholasa. **In Nueva York.** Dial, 1977; Arte Público Press, 1988.

Set on New York's Lower East Side, the stories in this collection of interrelated short stories affirm the strength of the human spirit that grows no matter what the circumstances. This book is for more mature readers.

1. Read aloud the chapter introducing "Old Mary." Nicholasa Mohr has said that she experienced similar incidents when she was 9 years old. Her aunt was deaf (and wouldn't wear a hearing aid) and played the numbers. Write a short character sketch about an interesting person you know. Make sure to use descriptive language, and the incidents you recount should reflect the nature of the person's personality.

2. How is Aunt Mary different from or the same as one of your aunts?

Mohr, Nicholasa. **El Bronx Remembered.** Harper, 1975; Arte Público Press, 1985.

A collection of stories about life in El Bronx, the Puerto Rican barrio in New York City in the 1950s, the decade of the largest Puerto Rican influx. The stories, which are for more mature readers, range from funny to sad. Have students do the following.

1. Read one or more stories. After reading each one, make a list of things you think happen because the characters are Puerto Rican in heritage, because they are living in the 1950s, or because they are living in New York.

2. If the people in Nicholasa Mohr's books were living in the 1990s, how do you think their lives would be different?

Mohr, Nicholasa. **Nilda.** Harper, 1973; Arte Público Press, 1986.

Nilda lives in El Barrio, the Spanish Harlem, in New York City. The entire novel focuses on life in the 1940s. Written in a narrative journal format, the episodes give an intimate glimpse of life inside the barrio. For mature readers.

1. Make a list of the characters in this book and connect them with lines indicating relationships. These relationships might be formal or informal.

2. Discuss how life in the 1940s was different from life in the 1990s. How did this story indicate the setting in terms of time?

3. Read one of Lois Lowry's novels about Anastasia and compare the life that is portrayed in her book with life as it is portrayed in Mohr's book.

FURTHER READING

After World War I, Puerto Ricans who could afford the freighter fare came to the United States, many as skilled cigarmakers. Pedro and Nicholasa Golpé and their sons came to the United States several years after that, just before the beginning of World War II. At the time, the economic situation in Puerto Rico was devastating—much worse than any of the considerable hardships the Golpé family had to face in the United States. They had dreams that with hard work they could create opportunities and offer their children a decent education and a good life. Mohr says, "No one leaves their homeland to freeze in the winter and sizzle in the summer." Her family hoped for something better than what they had. Discuss with students why people emigrate to the United States. Discuss political and economic conditions that bring people to this country. Read other books about immigrants. The following are fiction books or photoessays about immigrants and their experiences in the United States.

- Freedman, Russell. *Immigrant Kids*. Illustrated with photographs. Dutton, 1980.

- Gilson, Jamie. *Hello, My Name Is Scrambled Eggs*. Lothrop, 1985.

- Hewett, Joan. *Hector Lives in the United States Now*. Illustrated by Richard R. Hewett. Lippincott, 1990.

- Levitin, Sonia. *Journey to America*. Illustrated by Charles Robinson. Aladdin, 1970.

A more comprehensive booklist and activities relating to immigration and family heritage can be located in chapter 3, "We All Came (Coming to America)," in *Adventures with Social Studies (Through Literature)* by Sharron McElmeel (Libraries Unlimited, 1991).

Brian Pinkney

From *Bookpeople: A Multicultural Album* by Sharron L. McElmeel (Libraries Unlimited, Inc., 1992)

·illustrator·illustrator·illustrator·

Brian Pinkney

Jerry Brian Pinkney, known as Brian Pinkney, grew up in an artistic family. His mother, Gloria Pinkney, is a children's book writer, and his father is the award-winning illustrator Jerry Pinkney. A brother is an art director for an advertising agency.

Jerry Brian Pinkney was born August 28, 1961, in Boston, Massachusetts. Later his family moved to Croton-on-Hudson, New York. During his growing-up years he spent summers on Cape Cod. He explored New England's shores, attended African dance concerts, visited zoos, drew things he saw, and made his own toys. Creating art was part of his life. After attending art school, Brian Pinkney worked in an art supply store while he tried to sell his artwork. During the time he was teaching drawing to children at the Children's Art Carnival in Harlem, an art director saw his work in *Cricket Magazine* and contacted him about illustrating *The Boy and the Ghost*. When he started illustrating books, he used watercolor but now he often uses "scratchboard," a technique in which black ink is scratched off a white board to create an image.

When he needs a break from his work, he often "drums" on the back of his chair. He also practices Tae Kwon Do to work off energy. On his list of favorite things are chicken and the color blue. On October 12, 1991, Brian Pinkney married Andrea R. Davis, a children's book writer. They live in Brooklyn, New York.

Brian Pinkney

ABOUT THE ILLUSTRATOR

Jerry Brian Pinkney was born August 28, 1961, in Boston, Massachusetts. The Pinkney family moved to Croton-on-Hudson, New York, where Brian's life was filled with activity. He spent much of his growing-up time exploring the shores of Cape Cod, where the family spent summers. His parents, Jerry and Gloria Pinkney, still live in Croton-on-Hudson. Gloria Pinkney is a children's book writer, and Jerry Pinkney is a well-known illustrator. He illustrated *Mirandy and Brother Wind* by Patricia McKissack (Knopf, 1988) and *The Talking Eggs* by Robert D. San Souci (Dial, 1989). Jerry Pinkney is also an associate professor of art at the University of Delaware.

When Brian was a child and attended African dance concerts or zoos, he would often come home and draw what he had seen. His mother encouraged him to show his artwork to his father, who always complimented his son on his work. Brian, who wanted to be a drummer when he grew up, played in marching, jazz, and rock bands. He also channeled his energy into the study of Tae Kwon Do.

Brian Pinkney attended his father's alma mater, the Philadelphia College of Art, and earned a Bachelor of Fine Arts degree. He then returned to the New York City area to attend the School of Visual Arts, where he earned a Master of Fine Arts. For a time he worked in an art supply store while he attempted to sell his artwork. During the years he was doing graduate work, he was also teaching painting and drawing to under-privileged children at the Children's Art Carnival in Harlem. Besides teaching he was doing a lot of textbook and magazine illustrating. It was during those years that an editor at Simon & Schuster approached him about illustrating a children's book, an African-American story. The editor had seen some of Pinkney's work published in *Cricket Magazine* and liked what she saw. The manuscript she offered him was Robert D. San Souci's *The Boy and the Ghost*. Brian's father had read the story earlier and had decided that he was not interested in illustrating it, but Brian saw himself as a little boy in the story. He accepted the project and set out to find a little boy to use as a model. He searched for a little boy that reminded him of himself as a child. After accepting the project, he researched rural southern settings. The research interested him because it related to his life and his heritage. He always wants to know more about himself and about things that help him understand his past and his place in society. Pinkney feels that illustrating books that feature Black characters gives him an opportunity to present a positive image of Blacks, a truthful and nonstereotypic image. Some of the stories he has illustrated—for example, *The Ballad of Belle Dorcas* and *A Wave in Her Pocket: Stories from Trinidad*—are clearly stories that come from the African experience. But some of his more recent illustrations, such as for *Where Does the Trail Lead?*, are for stories that could have been illustrated with images of children of any nationality. He chooses to illustrate them with Black characters simply because there is a need for such books.

His first book, *The Boy and the Ghost*, is an African-American ghost story set at the turn of the century. Pinkney illustrated the book with line-and-water-color drawings (similar to the style used by his father). For *The Ballad of Belle Dorcas* he used a "scratchboard" technique, in which a white board is coated with black ink and the ink is then scratched or etched off with a sharp tool. Careful planning lets the desired image emerge from the white underneath. It is primarily a black-and-white technique, but Pinkney has elevated it to one that uses muted colors to enhance the images. Earlier technique dictated that separate scratchboards had to be produced for each color, but it seems that now the underlayer can be various colors (not just white), and the full-color art can be reproduced photographically. Pinkney compares this technique to "sculpting the image as well as drawing it." He feels that the scratchboard technique allows him to show a lot of energy and movement in his illustrations. *Where Does the Trail Lead?* allowed him to return to his childhood memories of summers on Cape Cod. He again used scratchboard to illustrate the story of a young boy's adventures by the sea.

Brian Pinkney's work has appeared in The *New York Times Magazine*, *Woman's Day*, *Business Tokyo*, *Ebony Man*, and *Instructor* magazine. In 1990 he exhibited at the Original Art Show at the Society of Illustrators and had a solo exhibition at the School of Visual Arts Student Galleries. Also in 1990 Brian Pinkney was honored with The National Arts Club Award of Distinction.

On October 12, 1991, J. Brian Pinkney married Andrea R. Davis, a children's book author. They live in Brooklyn where he enjoys practicing Tae Kwon Do and working on his illustrations projects.

THE BOOKSHELF

For the reader's convenience, the following activity section is arranged in alphabetical order by author's last name.

Albert, Burton. **Where Does the Trail Lead?** Illustrated by Brian Pinkney. Simon, 1991.

Memories of summer days at Cape Cod were Pinkney's inspiration as he created the illustrations for this book. It is the story of a boy who follows a trail through buttercups, snapdragons, sand, and crunchy pine needles. He climbs over dunes and past honking geese — enjoying the smell of the salty sea. Pinkney's scratchboard illustrations show a young Black boy enjoying ordinary activities on Summertime Island.

1. Explore the theme of island life by introducing students to the following books.

   Brown, Margaret Wise. *The Little Island*. Illustrated by Leonard Weisgard. Doubleday, 1946. (1947 Caldecott Medal)

   Cooney, Barbara. *Island Boy*. Illustrated by Barbara Cooney. Viking, 1988.

   _____. *Miss Rumphius*. Illustrated by Barbara Cooney. Viking, 1982.

   Lasky, Kathryn. *My Island Grandma*. Illustrated by Emily Arnold McCully. Warne, 1979.

   McCloskey, Robert. *One Morning in Maine*. Illustrated by Robert McCloskey. Viking, 1952.

   _____. *Time of Wonder*. Illustrated by Robert McCloskey. Viking, 1957; reissued 1989. (1958 Caldecott Medal)

2. Have students compare the illustrations in this book with the scratchboard illustrated created by Barbara Cooney for *Chanticleer and the Fox* (Crowell, 1958) and several of Leonard Everett Fisher's illustrated titles, including *The First Book Edition of Casey at the Bat* by Ernest L. Thayer (Watts, 1965), and Fisher's own titles in the Colonial American Craftsman Series, including *The Silversmiths* (Watts, 1965), *The Papermakers* (Watts, 1965), *The Hatters* (Watts, 1965), and *The Wigmakers* (Watts, 1965).

Hooks, William H. **The Ballad of Belle Dorcas.** Illustrated by Brian Pinkney. Knopf, 1990.

A free-issue African American, Belle Dorcas, falls in love with, Joshua, a slave. When she realizes that he might be sold away, she consults a conger (conjure) woman to obtain a spell that will save him. The spell keeps him from being sold, but he is imprisoned as a cedar tree. Later when the cedar tree is cut down, he becomes part of the smokehouse that the tree is used to build. When Belle Dorcas dies, the smokehouse disappears. And when the story ends, "Two young cedar trees were found growing side by side."

1. The illustrations in this book are fine examples of Pinkney's scratchboard technique. Have students emulate this technique by following the steps below:

    a. Color a sheet of white paper with a thick layer of color. Or use a white crayon if you prefer a black-and-white picture. If you want colors to show through, color bands of various colors across the width of the paper.

    b. Cover the entire paper with a thick coat of black crayon.

    c. Use a round toothpick or any pointed object to scratch (or etch) out a drawing. As you scratch through the black layer, the underlayer of white or color will show through.

2. The Author's Note at the beginning of the book explains the terms "free-issue" and "conjure/conger" and the origin of this tale. A discussion of these terms and the conditions that were prevalent during the days African Americans were held as slaves could help students better understand attitudes people hold today. Read the notes and discuss the attitudes held during the years prior to the Civil War.

    a. Further older students' understanding of the conditions endured by slaves by reading one or more of the slave stories told by Julius Lester. See index.

    b. The conjure woman is a minor character in Patricia McKissack's *Mirandy and Brother Wind.* Use that character to connect Hooks's story with McKissack's tale of a girl who attempts to capture Brother Wind. See index.

3. There actually is a Joshua tree. Research information about that tree and see if it could possibly be the tree spoken of in *The Ballad of Belle Dorcas.* Explain why or why not.

Joseph, Lynn. **A Wave in Her Pocket: Stories from Trinidad.** Illustrated by Brian Pinkney. Clarion, 1991.

Tantie is a storyteller who has a story for every occasion. In this collection she tells Amber and her cousins stories—some scary, some funny. One is about Soucouyant, who leaves her skin in a stone jug and flies by night to attack her villagers; another one, about Amber and her mother, is funny. These original stories are based on traditional folklore and humor from the author's memories of her own island childhood.

1. Locate Trinidad on a map and gather and share some information about that area of the world. Trinidad is the setting for the story and also the author's childhood home.

2. After collecting some information about Trinidad, look at Pinkney's illustrations to ascertain the authenticity of his images. Did he accurately represent Trinidad? Why or why not?

3. Storytellers are commonplace in many cultures. Gail E. Haley uses Aunt Poppy as a storyteller in *Jack and the Bean Tree* (Crown, 1986) and *Jack and the Fire Dragon* (Crown, 1988). Richard Chase uses a storyteller in *The Jack Tales* (Houghton, 1943) and *Grandfather Tales* (Houghton, 1948). Compare the characteristics of the three storytellers.

Knudson, R. R. **Julie Brown: Racing against the World.** Illustrated by J. Brian Pinkney. Viking, 1988. (Women of Our Time™)

This is a courageous story of triumph over challenges facing women in sports today. Julie Brown succeeded in representing the United States in the 1984 Olympics in spite of pressure to use illegal drugs for bodybuilding, the 1980 Olympic boycott, and repeated injuries.

1. Julie Brown is just one of the heroes profiled in this series; she is also included in other biographies about notable role models. Focus on biographies of people who will inspire readers to set goals and to take advantage of opportunities. Suggested subjects follow.

John James Audubon	Arthur Mitchell
Clara Barton	Grandma Moses
Mary McLeod Bethune	Martina Navratilova
Carol Burnett	Eleanor Roosevelt
Rachel Carson	Beverly Sills
Babe Didrikson	Henrietta Szold
Charles Eastman	Maria Tallchief
Betty Friedan	Mother Teresa
Susan LaFlesche	Margaret Thatcher
Dorothea Lange	Jim Thorpe
Juliette Gordon Low	Eddie Van Halen
Malcom X	Lillian Wald
Margaret Mead	Andrew Young
Golda Meir	

2. Discuss with students the qualities that help a person to succeed. What defines success?

San Souci, Robert D. **The Boy and the Ghost.** Illustrated by J. Brian Pinkney. Simon, 1989.

Thomas, the middle child of 7 children in a poor African-American family, meets a stranger on the way to look for a job. This stranger, a ghost, has a treasure he'll give Thomas—but only on certain terms. Pinkney's line-and-watercolor drawings are inspired. Scenes showing the hot fields and the family's poor shanty are quiet and calm, but scenes involving the ghost are filled with action.

1. Compare and contrast this story with Sibyl Hancock's *Esteban and the Ghost* (Dutton, 1983). The setting is different and some of the details are changed. Using a story grammar chart for each story will help (see appendix A).

2. Another tale with similarities in story grammar is Anne Rockwell's *The Bump in the Night* (Green-willow, 1979). Rockwell's tale is based on a Spanish folktale. Use the story grammar chart in Appendix A to help compare and contrast this story with San Souci's.

3. Natalie Savage Carlson has written a tale that shares some elements with San Souci's story. Read *The Ghost in the Lagoon*, illustrated by Andrew Glass (Lothrop, 1984). Glass's illustrations are created with cross-hatching. Compare the story text to San Souci's and Pinkney's scratchboard illustrations to Glass's cross-hatching.

4. Older readers will enjoy reading or hearing ghost story selections by Jane Yolen and Martin H. Greenberg from *Things That Go Bump in the Night* (Harper, 1989).

FURTHER READING

J. Brian Pinkney is the son of award-winning illustrator Jerry Pinkney, who often uses African-American characters when he illustrates books. To learn more about Jerry Pinkney, use the video profile *Meet the Caldecott Illustrator: Jerry Pinkney*. This 21-minute presentation, available from American School Publishers, deals mostly with Pinkney's illustrative technique and is most appropriate for late primary, intermediate, or middle/junior high school students. Also, have students read books illustrated by Jerry Pinkney.

Books Illustrated by Jerry Pinkney

Aardema, Verna. *Ji-nongo-nongo Means Riddles*. Four Winds, 1978.

Adoff, Arnold. *In for Winter, Out for Spring*. Harcourt, 1991.

Carlstrom, Nancy White. *Wild Wild Sunflower Child Anna*. Macmillan, 1987.

Dragonwagon, Crescent. *Half a Moon and One Whole Star*. Macmillan, 1986.

Fields, Julia. *The Great Lion of Zion Street*. McElderry, 1988.

Martel, Cruz. *Yagua Days*. Dial, 1976.

McKissack, Patricia. *Mirandy and Brother Wind*. Knopf, 1988. (Caldecott honor book)

Robinson, Adjai. *Femi and Old Grandaddie*. Coward, 1972.

Saleh, Harold J. *Even Tiny Ants Must Sleep*. McGraw, 1967.

San Souci, Robert D. *The Talking Eggs: A Folktale from the American South*. Dial, 1989.

Zaslavsky, Claudia. *Count on Your Fingers African Style*. Crowell, 1980.

Brian Pinkney often uses Black children in his illustrations for books that deal with experiences any child could have, because there is such a need for books with Black children in them. Children of all races need to see that Black children are part of the mainstream of life. Introduce students to other books in which Black children are featured.

Books with Black Characters

Alexander, Martha. *Sabrina.* Illustrated by Martha Alexander. Pied Piper, 1991.

Bang, Molly. *Ten, Nine, Eight.* Illustrated by Molly Bang. Greenwillow, 1983.

_____. *Wiley and the Hairy Man.* Illustrated by Molly Bang. Macmillan, 1976.

Berry, James. *A Thief in the Village and Other Stories of Jamaica.* Puffin, 1990.

_____. *When I Dance.* Illustrated by Karen Barbour. Harcourt, 1991.

Blume, Judy. *Iggie's House.* Bradbury, 1970.

Brown, Marcia. *Shadow.* Illustrated by Marcia Brown. Scribner, 1982.

Craft, Ruth. *The Day of the Rainbow.* Illustrated by Niki Daly. Viking, 1989.

Daly, Niki. *Not So Fast, Songololo.* Illustrated by Niki Daly. McElderry, 1982.

Fenner, Carol. *The Skates of Uncle Richard.* Illustrated by Ati Forberg. Random, 1978.

Fox, Paula. *How Many Miles to Babylon?* Illustrated by Paul Giovanopoulos. Bradbury, 1980.

Greenfield, Eloise. *Night on Neighborhood Street.* Illustrated by Jan Spivey Gilchrist. Dial, 1991.

Hamilton, Virginia. *Zeely.* Illustrated by Symeon Shimin. Macmillan, 1967.

Hoffman, Mary. *Amazing Grace.* Illustrated by Caroline Binch. Dial, 1991.

Howard, Elizabeth Fitzgerald. *Aunt Flossie's Hats (And Crab Cakes Later).* Illustrated by James Ransome. Clarion, 1991.

_____. *The Train to Lulu's.* Illustrated by Robert Casilla. Bradbury, 1988.

Irwin, Hadley. *I Be Somebody.* McElderry, 1984.

Jones, Rebecca C. *Matthew and Tilly.* Illustrated by Beth Peck. Dutton, 1991.

Keats, Ezra Jack. *Goggles.* Illustrated by Ezra Jack Keats. Macmillan, 1969.

_____. *Hi, Cat!* Illustrated by Ezra Jack Keats. Macmillan, 1970.

_____. *Pet Show!* Illustrated by Ezra Jack Keats. Macmillan, 1972.

_____. *A Snowy Day.* Illustrated by Ezra Jack Keats. Viking, 1962; Puffin, 1977.

_____. *Whistle for Willie.* Illustrated by Ezra Jack Keats. Viking, 1962; Puffin, 1976.

Mathis, Sharon Bell. *The Hundred Penny Box.* Illustrated by Leo Dillon and Diane Dillon. Viking, 1975; Puffin, 1986.

Mayer, Mercer. *Liza Lou and the Yeller Belly Swamp.* Illustrated by Mercer Mayer. Four Winds, 1980.

Meyers, Susan. *Insect Zoo*. Illustrated by Richard Hewett. Lodestar, 1991.

Miles, Betty. *Sink or Swim*. Knopf, 1986.

Seeger, Pete. *Abiyoyo*. Illustrated by Michael Hays. Macmillan, 1985.

Turner, Ann. *Nettie's Trip South*. Illustrated by Ronald Himler. Macmillan, 1987.

Walker, Alice. *To Hell with Dying*. Illustrated by Catherine Deeter. Harcourt, 1988.

Wallin, Luke. *The Slavery Ghosts*. Bradbury, 1985.

Walter, Mildred Pitts. *Mariah Loves Rock*. Bradbury, 1988.

Winter, Jeanette. *Follow the Drinking Gourd*. Illustrated by Jeanette Winter. Knopf, 1988.

Virginia
Driving Hawk Sneve

From *Bookpeople: A Multicultural Album* by Sharron L. McElmeel (Libraries Unlimited, Inc., 1992)

Virginia Driving Hawk Sneve

Virginia Driving Hawk Sneve describes her childhood as "happy and secure.... We were poor, but I didn't know that because so was everyone else on the reservation." She was born on the Rosebud Indian Reservation in South Dakota on February 21, 1934. She attended Bureau of Indian Affairs schools until sixth grade, when she went to a school for Indian girls in Springfield, South Dakota. As a student she was encouraged to read beyond the small school library, and she was encouraged to write. Her father was a Sioux Episcopal priest. Once, an eastern church congregation sent a box of rummage to her family's rectory home, and she found books by Louisa May Alcott. Jo from *Little Women* set her to writing. After attending South Dakota State University, she became an educator and later a newspaper editor.

Through her writing Virginia Driving Hawk Sneve attempts to give an accurate picture of Native-American life. Her published works include novels and a collection of Native-American poetry. She and her husband, Vance M. Sneve, live in Rapid City, South Dakota. They have one daughter, Shirley, two sons, Paul and Alan, and four grandchildren, Joan, Bonita, Madeline, and Nickolas. Some of her favorite things are prime rib, spinach salad, the color teal blue or aqua, her grandchildren, and the Black Hills. When she is not writing or not in school, she plays the piano, gardens in the summer, and quilts in the winter.

Virginia Driving Hawk Sneve

ABOUT THE AUTHOR

Virginia Driving Hawk Sneve (pronounced "Snavy") was born on February 21, 1934, on the Rosebud Indian Reservation in South Dakota. She is an enrolled member of the Sioux tribe. Her parents were James H. Driving Hawk and Rose Driving Hawk. Her father, a Sioux Episcopal priest, was her hero during her growing-up years. He sang, played the saxophone, and taught her how to dance, drive a car, and hunt pheasants. He stressed education as being the only way Native Americans would be able to survive in the modern world. In one of the rectories where the family lived, Virginia found a set of the *Book of Knowledge* and other books, which she described as "a treasure of world literature." She devoured the stories and poems. Another time she found a set of Louisa May Alcott's books among the rummage sent by an eastern congregation. Virginia attended Bureau of Indian Affairs schools until sixth grade, when she went to St. Mary's School for Indian Girls in Springfield, South Dakota. Her teachers often gave her books and encouraged her to read beyond what was available in the small school library. Teachers at St. Mary's also encouraged her to write.

Virginia's father died when she was 14, but his belief in the value of education inspired her to continue her education beyond high school. She attended South Dakota State University, where she earned her first degree in 1954, and a master's in education in 1965. She taught English in public schools in White and Pierre, South Dakota, and then worked with Native Americans in the Flandreau Indian School in Flandreau, South Dakota, first as an English teacher and then as a guidance counselor. In the 1970s she began working as an editor for the Brevet Press in Sioux Falls. She is now a counselor working with Native-American youth in the Rapid City, South Dakota, public schools.

Whether she is working as an editor, writer, or educator, Virgina Driving Hawk Sneve strives to correct inaccurate information about Native Americans. She is one of the very few Native Americans who has written for children, although there are many Native-American writers who write for adults. Sneve was able to take advantage of that fact when she entered a contest sponsored by the Interracial Council of Minority Books for Children. Her manuscript, *Jimmy Yellow Hawk*, won that contest, in the Native-American category.

Sneve's novels reflect the spirit of the Native American's existence. Historical events, such as the Battle of the Little Big Horn and the 1862 uprising, are part of her stories, but each is brought into the present day through Sneve's fictionalized dialogue and incidents. She has also collected poems of young Native Americans in a book titled *Dancing Teepees*, illustrated by Stephen Gammell. Her novels were illustrated by Chief Oren Lyons, a member of the Turtle Clan of the Onondaga Nation. At the time he illustrated the books, he was living on the Onondaga reservation in Nedrow, New York. He was also an associate professor in American studies at the State University of New York at Buffalo. Some of his work was painted on hand-tanned elkhide; other of his illustrations are pen-and-ink drawings. Sneve discussed the illustrator for *Dancing Teepees* in an interview in May 1991, "Stephen Gammell is the only non-Indian who has illustrated my books. His illustrations for *Dancing Teepees* are beautiful and true to the Native-American artistic tradition. The soft, near pastel colors he used are like the traditional subdued native colors because they were made from natural elements—roots, berries, bark, etc.—not the bright colors of chemically produced oils or acrylics."

Sneve's novels were published in the 1970s and are out of print, but she still gets letters from children of all races who tell her how much they like them. Some want to come visit the reservation and meet the characters from the books, and Native-American children write to tell her how much they like reading about places and people that are like places and people they know. Her collection of poetry is a current publication, and she is working on a photoessay book about the Lakota Name Ceremony for Lerner Publications. She is also working on a historical exploration of her "Indian great-great grandmothers—placing their oral history within the written." This book will be an adult title.

Virginia Driving Hawk Sneve has been married for 35 years. Her husband, Vance, is her best friend. Their daughter, Shirley, has two daughters, Joan (1980) and Bonita (1990). Their first son, Paul, has two children, Nickolas (1983) and Madeline (1986). Alan, the youngest child, is a student at the University of Minnesota. The Sneves often attend concerts and plays in the school and the community. They enjoy the Black Hills area where they live and the time they spend with their grandchildren.

THE BOOKSHELF

Sneve, Virginia Driving Hawk. **Betrayed.** Illustrated by Oren Lyons. Holiday, 1974.

The background for this story is the broken promises of U.S. government Indian agents—broken promises that brought about the 1862 Sioux uprising. The starving Santee tribe raid a settlement at Lake Shetek and take prisoners. Among them are Sarah, her mother, her sister, and neighbors. While the prisoners are wandering through the Dakota Territory with their Indian captors, Waanatan, of the Teton tribe, tracks down the fugitive tribesmen and rescues the captive women and children by bartering guns, horses, and blankets. In an author's note Sneve states that she retained the true names of the characters and places and followed as closely as possible the actual historical evidence in the 1862 incident. But she used her imagination to develop the characters, dialogue, and situations.

1. The Trail of the Shetek Captives extended north from Lake Shetek (near the southern border of Minnesota and the northern Iowa border) to Elm River in North Dakota, southwest to the North Dakota–South Dakota border, northwest to the place where the Beaver Creek joins the Missouri River, south along the Missouri River to Fort Primeau in South Dakota, and south to Fort Randall near the Missouri River on the Nebraska–South Dakota border. Plot the trail of the captives on a map.

2. Use reference books to locate historical information about the Santees or Tetons and the 1862 Sioux uprising. Checking the indexes of books that deal with Native Americans will facilitate the search. Take notes from each source and compile and share the information.

Sneve, Virginia Driving Hawk. **Dancing Teepees: Poems of American Indian Youth.** Illustrated by Steven Gammell. Holiday, 1989.

This collection contains nineteen poetic verses from various Native-American traditions: Apache, Paiute, Mescalero Apache, Hopi, Dakota, Navajo, Ute-Navajo, Zuni, Omaha, Wintu, Lakota Sioux, Osage, and Crow. The book contains some original poems in the Native-American tradition by Sneve.

1. Read aloud one of these poems each day until all nineteen have been read. Locate the traditional homes of all the tribes mentioned, and determine where those tribes are today.

2. Sneve's poetic selections are based on Native-American traditions. Other traditions, including story-telling, have been passed down from generation to generation. In Diane Hoyt-Goldsmith's *Pueblo*

Storyteller (Holiday, 1991) 10-year-old April shares some Pueblo traditions. Discuss these traditions and compare them to the students' own traditions.

Sneve, Virginia Driving Hawk. **High Elk's Treasure.** Illustrated by Oren Lyons. Holiday, 1972.

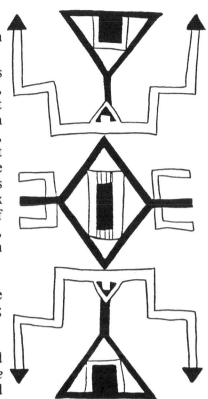

This story takes place in a contemporary setting. Joe High Elk and his sister, Marie, find the cave where their ancestor, Steps High Like an Elk, hid his palomino mare from thieving white soldiers. It was this mare that began High Elk's renowned herd of horses. While in this cave, the children find a "treasure" they think was put there by their ancestor. The treasure, wrapped in moldering leather, is almost a hundred years old. The secret that the document holds relates to General Custer and the Battle of the Little Big Horn. In an author's note, Sneve states that all the characters are fictitious, with the exception of Custer, his brother, and the Sioux warrior Rain-in-the-Face. And although the story uncovers the mystery of who actually killed Custer (how he died has never been authenticated), Sneve says she does not purport to have any new or specific information about Custer's death.

1. Read a historical account of the Battle of the Little Big Horn. One source is Quentin Reynolds's *Custer's Last Stand* (Random, 1951; 1987).

2. Correlate activities with this title to those suggested for Paul and Dorothy Goble's *Red Hawk's Account of Custer's Last Battle: The Battle of the Little Big Horn, 25 June 1876* (Pantheon, 1969; reissued University of Nebraska Press, 1992). See index.

Sneve, Virginia Driving Hawk. **Jimmy Yellow Hawk.** Illustrated by Oren Lyons. Holiday, 1972.

James Henry Yellow Hawk does not like his nickname, "Little Jim." In the old days, a Sioux boy earned his nickname by some deed of valor. But his grandfather tells him that a name can also be earned through some disgrace. So "Little Jim" has a great deal of growing up to do before his father speaks of him as "my son, Jimmy." Set in the background of this story is the excitement of the rodeo, a lost mare in a dangerous storm, and a tribal dance contest.

1. The Dakota Creek Reservation in this book is a fictional place. The author states that it "could be any one of the western South Dakota reservations." Help students locate the existing reservations on a map of South Dakota.

2. The author uses actual family names of Indians on South Dakota Indian reservations, but the story is fictionalized. After locating the reservations as suggested in activity 1, have students write to a student at an elementary or middle/junior high school on one of the reservations. Call information for phone numbers and call the schools for names and addresses. The goal would be to establish a pen-pal relationship.

Sneve, Virginia Driving Hawk. **When Thunder Spoke.** Illustrated by Oren Lyons. Holiday, 1974.

Norman Two Bull's family has lived on the Dakota (Sioux) Reservation for three generations. His mother wears contemporary clothing and seems to disapprove of Norman's grandfather, Matt Two Bull, who clings to traditional ways. Valuable agates and a relic found on sacred land create the impression that traditional beliefs are still valued.

1. Hold a class debate on whether it would make good sense to establish a quarry at Thunder Butte.

2. Discuss the relationship between Norman, his mother, and his grandfather, Matt Two Bull.

FURTHER READING

Virginia Driving Hawk Sneve is one of a very few Native Americans who writes contemporary fiction for children. While her novels, written in the 1970s, are currently out of print, they are worth searching out. If your students think these books should be more available, they might wish to start a campaign to get them back into print so that they would be more available to readers. As a motivational example, share the story of Annie Bronn Johnston, who led the fight to save the wild mustangs. Marguerite Henry wrote an account of her campaign in *Mustang, Wild Spirit of the West* (Rand McNally, 1971). "Wild Horse Annie" led the fight to save the mustangs and, as a result of the publicity generated by Henry's book, hundreds of school children wrote letters to the Secretary of the Interior urging that a permanent refuge be established for the wild horses in the Bookcliff Mountains of Colorado, near the Utah border. Their campaign was successful, and protective legislation was passed. Henry's book shows the power of individuals banding together to accomplish a goal.

Perhaps a letter-writing campaign to Holiday House might bring about the reissue of Sneve's novels. Another goal might be to convince publishers that children of all races would like to read stories—authentic stories—about children of many different cultures. The list of publishers' addresses that appears in appendix B of this book might be useful in corresponding with acquisitions editors for children's books at publishing houses.

Yoshiko Uchida

Yoshiko Uchida

From *Bookpeople: A Multicultural Album* by Sharron L. McElmeel (Libraries Unlimited, Inc., 1992)

Yoshiko Uchida

Yoshiko Uchida remembers the days during World War II when her family was held in concentration camps, where Americans of Japanese heritage were sent after the bombing of Pearl Harbor. She wrote a book about those years, *Journey to Topaz: A Story of the Japanese-American Evacuation.* She has written many others that retell Japanese folktales or are stories about Japanese Americans.

Yoshiko Uchida was born on November 24, 1921, in Alameda, California. She grew up in Berkeley, California. Her father, Dwight Takashi Uchida, was a businessman. Her mother, Iku Uchida, was a poet. Yoshiko wanted to be a writer, too. She wrote her first book on brown wrapping paper when she was 10, and on the day she finished elementary school, she began a "Journal of Special Events." When she grew up she taught elementary school for a short time, but teaching did not give her enough time for writing. So she got a secretarial job and spent her evenings writing. She has been a full-time writer for many years.

Yoshiko Uchida likes Japanese food, especially sushi and chicken teriyaki. She enjoys reading, painting, and taking leisure walks. Because of a chronic illness, she has not been able to go to the theater or to travel as often as she would like. She lives in Berkeley.

Yoshiko Uchida

ABOUT THE AUTHOR

Yoshiko Uchida (Oo-chee-dah) was born November 24, 1921, in Alameda, California. Her father, Dwight Takashi Uchida, was a businessman in San Francisco. Her mother, Iku Uchida, wrote poetry. The family lived in Berkeley, California, in a small house with a large yard. Her mother cooked Japanese foods and Japanese was spoken at home. Yoshiko and her older sister sometimes wore kimonos for special programs at school. On the third day of March, the family celebrated Dolls Festival Day. A tea party would be held to show off special dolls put on display. The family had many books from Japan, and stories from those books were often read to Yoshiko and her sister. The Uchidas even traveled to Japan one year.

Yoshiko also read Louisa May Alcott's *Little Women* and *Little Men*, Frances H. Hodgson's *The Secret Garden*, and Anna Sewell's *Black Beauty*. And as a young writer, she often wrote her stories on brown wrapping paper.

Yoshiko attended school in Berkeley and was a senior at the University of California at Berkeley when Pearl Harbor was bombed in December 1941. All Japanese in the United States, even if they were born in this country and were U.S. citizens, were ordered to leave their homes and to go to relocation centers (now referred to by historians as concentration camps). At first the Uchidas were sent to live in a horse stall at the Tanforan Race Track. They were held there for 5 months and then sent to a guarded camp, Topaz, in the Utah desert. Yoshiko received her diploma, by mail, in a cardboard roll. She taught second-grade children at Topaz during the year her family spent in that camp. After receiving a fellowship to study at Smith College, Yoshiko was released. Her family was released that same year.

Yoshiko earned her master's degree and started her teaching career in a Quaker school near Philadelphia. She moved to New York City and worked as a secretary while she tried to write stories and articles. In 1952 the Ford Foundation granted her a fellowship to travel to Japan so that she could collect material for more books. She was to spend one year in Japan, but she liked it so much she stayed for a second year. While in Japan she was able to collect folktales and study folk art. When she returned to the United States, she became the West Coast correspondent for *Craft Horizons* magazine. She lived for a while in Oakland and eventually began to write full time. She wrote stories for many magazines, including *Woman's Day*, the magazine that first accepted one of her stories. Her first children's book, *The Dancing Kettle and Other Japanese Folk Tales*, was published in 1949.

Uchida's earlier stories focused on stories from Japan. Her first three books were collections of Japanese folktales. After the death of her mother in 1966, Uchida wanted to write a book for her parents, a book that would reflect and acknowledge the hardships that all first-generation Japanese had gone through. That book, *Journey to Topaz: A Story of the Japanese-American Evacuation*, became an account of her own family's experiences in the World War II camps. The story is told through the eyes of 11-year-old Yuki. Uchida continues Yuki's story in *Journey Home*, which tells of the Sakane family's return to Berkeley, in an aura of hostility. The family goes into partnership with other Japanese Americans and establishes a grocery store. Uchida says that this second story is not part of her own family's experiences, but it is reflective of the experiences of many Japanese people after they were released from the concentration camps.

In an interview in May 1991, Yoshiko Uchida said, "I've always loved children's books and wanted to share with American children the wonderful Japanese folk tales I'd heard as a child. Sharing stories, I hoped, would help them understand other cultures and see that people everywhere have the same hopes, fears, and joys." Writers often inject some of their own experiences into the books they write. Personalities of friends or acquaintances show up as characters in stories, and specific incidents reoccur on the pages of the books. Uchida talks about the pieces of her life that are in her books: "A good bit of me is in Rinko, the child in my trilogy. *A Jar of Dreams, The Best Bad Thing* and *The Happiest Ending*, although the stories are fictional and not about my family. Also, *Journey to Topaz* is based on my own experiences during World War II when we were interned by our government, so there is much of me in Yuki. Her story continues in *Journey Home*, but again, this is not about my family."

Uchida has been writing for more than 40 years. In the mid-1980s, she was diagnosed as having Chronic Fatigue Immune Dysfunction Syndrome, which has kept her from traveling and going to the theater. But she still enjoys reading, painting, and walking. In 1990 she was able to begin writing again, something she had not been able to do for much of the previous 5 years. Her favorite color is blue, and her favorite foods are Japanese dishes, especially sushi and chicken teriyaki. She would like to have a dog—she and her older sister had one when they were children—but cannot because she lives in an apartment. That apartment is in Berkeley, California, where she writes near a window with a view of the flowers and the bonsai tree on her patio. Among her honors is an award from the University of Oregon in 1981 for "having made a significant contribution to the cultural development of society ... and .. [helping] to bring about a greater understanding of the Japanese American culture." In 1991 Julian Messner/Silver Burdett published *The Invisible Thread: An Autobiography*, and soon she will have two picture books published. The tentative titles are *The Magic Purse*, to be published by McElderry, and *The Bracelet*, to be published by Philomel.

THE BOOKSHELF

Uchida, Yoshiko. **The Best Bad Thing.** McElderry, 1983.

Written in first person, this story is a sequel to *A Jar of Dreams.* Rinko's parents ask her to spend a month helping Mrs. Hata, a widow. Mrs. Hata is eccentric (or crazy depending on your viewpoint), and her two sons, Zem and Abu, are ill-behaved. Mrs. Hata's spirit begins to be broken by the misfortunes that befall the Hata family. Rinko's family steps in to help Mrs. Hata find a job and build her independence and self-assurance. The story is set in California in the 1930s. There are occasional references to the prejudice felt by Japanese Americans during that period.

1. Discuss whether or not you would have liked Zem or Abu. Why or why not?

2. The story depicts some of the prejudice present in California (and throughout the country) in the 1930s, before World War II. Make a list of the incidents you think were prejudicial, and write a short paragraph discussing whether or not these same events could happen today.

3. If a sequel were written for this book, what do you think Mrs. Hata's life would be like? What are some of the things you think would happen to her and her family?

Uchida, Yoshiko. **The Birthday Visitor.** Illustrated by Charles Robinson. Scribner, 1975.

Emi thinks that her seventh birthday is going to be spoiled now that a minister is arriving. The situation of boring (or potentially boring) adult visitors is a situation with which many young readers will be able to identify. The birthday turns out to be one of Emi's best-ever days, because of the special qualities of the guest. A look at an ordinary event in the life of a Japanese American.

1. Have a class discussion about birthday celebrations after reading some of the following books.

Birthdays—Celebrations

Blume, Judy. "Birthday Bash." In *Tales of a Fourth Grade Nothing.* Illustrated by Roy Doty. Dutton, 1972.

Hoban, Russell. *A Birthday for Frances.* Illustrated by Lillian Hoban. HarperCollins, 1968.

Hurwitz, Johanna. "The Birthday Party." In *Aldo Applesauce.* Illustrated by John Wallner. Morrow, 1979.

Ichikawa, Satomi. *Happy Birthday! A Book of Birthday Celebrations.* Philomel, 1988.

Livingston, Myra Cohn. *Happy Birthday.* Illustrated by Eric Blegvad. Harcourt, 1964.

Additional books and suggestions for extending the birthday theme are included in a chapter, "Book Tricks—From Alphabet to Do-Nothing," in *My Bag of Book Tricks* by Sharron McElmeel (Libraries Unlimited, 1989), pages 9-36

2. Have students make a birthday cake for Emi. They can paint it on a sheet of paper or make a real one in the cooking center.

3. Discuss the differences and similarities between the way Emi celebrated her birthday and the way the children in the class celebrate theirs.

Uchido, Yoshiko. **The Dancing Kettle and Other Japanese Folk Tales.** Illustrated by Richard C. Jones. Harcourt, 1949; reissued Creative Arts, 1986.

   Several folktales have been adapted and retold with directness and economy of words. The tales tell of royal beings, monsters, ogres, and gods.

"The Wedding of the Mouse"

1. Read the story "The Wedding of the Mouse" from the collection and then discuss the idea of "power" and who is the most powerful.

2. Compare/contrast this version of the tale with other versions.

Tales to Compare with "The Wedding of the Mouse"

Bulatkin, I. F. "The Match-making of a Mouse." In *Eurasian Folk and Fairy Tales.* Criterion, 1965.

Gackenbach, Dick. *The Perfect Mouse.* Illustrated by Dick Gackenbach. Macmillan, 1984.

Kimmel, Eric A. *The Greatest of All: A Japanese Folktale*. Illustrated by Giora Carmi. Holiday, 1991.

Morimoto Junko. *Mouse's Marriage*. Illustrated by Junko Morimoto. Viking, 1986; Puffin, 1988.

3. *The Wedding of the Rat Family*, retold by Carol Kendall and illustrated by James Watts (McElderry, 1988), is cited as a "traditional Chinese story." It bears striking similarity to Uchida's tale "The Wedding of the Mouse." Compare/contrast the tales. What is it about Kendall's version that makes it Chinese? What is it about Uchida's or Kimmel's version that makes it Japanese? Are the differences significant?

4. Continue the theme of power and the seemingly least significant having the most power by sharing Gerald McDermott's *The Stonecutter* (Viking, 1957). McDermott's book is a Japanese tale strikingly similar to a tale retold and illustrated by Pam Newton, *The Stonecutter: An Indian Folktale* (Putnam, 1990). Discuss the similarities.

"Momotaro: The Peach Boy"

In Japan there is a legend that a woman who was washing found a great peach in the water. She carried it home to her husband, who opened it and found inside a baby boy, whom they raised. The boy, Momotaro, repaid them by defeating the people of the Island of the Devil and giving them their treasure.

1. Compare/contrast this tale to any of the many versions of Hans Christian Andersen's "Thumbelina" or Beatrice Schenk deRegniers's *Penny* (Lothrop, 1987).

2. Compare/contrast "The Peach Boy" with *The Inch Boy*, a Japanese folktale retold and illustrated by Junko Morimoto (Puffin, 1988).

"The Tongue-Cut Sparrow"

1. Compare Uchida's retelling with *The Tongue-Cut Sparrow*, retold by Momoko Ishii, translated from the Japanese by Katherine Paterson, and illustrated by Suekichi Akaba (Lodestar, 1987).

Other titles in this book are "Urashima Taro and the Princess of the Sea," "Dancing Kettle," "Rabbit and Crocodile," and "Old Man with a Bump." Folktales often have parallel tales in other cultures. Discuss the basic motifs of the tales and compare/contrast them with those of other folktales you already know.

Uchida, Yoshiko. **The Forever Christmas Tree.** Illustrated by Mizumura. Scribner, 1963.

A Christmas celebration among people who do not worship in the Christian manner brings home the spirit of a meaningful holiday. The story concerns the contagious spirit of Christmas that enables children to bring happiness to an old man.

1. Continue the spirit of giving during the holiday season by reading aloud selected stories from Katherine Paterson's *Angels and Other Strangers: Family Christmas Stories* (Crowell, 1979).

2. Share Barbara Robinson's *The Best Christmas Pageant Ever* (HarperCollins, 1972).

3. One book that subtly deals with the belief in the spirit of Christmas giving is Chris Van Allsburg's *The Polar Express* (Houghton, 1985). Before reading the story, ring a jingle bell to establish who can hear the bell. Share the story and repeat the bell ringing. How many can hear the ringing now? What does it mean?

Uchida, Yoshiko. **The Happiest Ending.** McElderry, 1985.

This is the third book in a trilogy that begins with *A Jar of Dreams* and *The Best Bad Thing*. In this final tale, 12-year-old Rinko finds out that a neighbor's daughter is coming from Japan to marry a man twice her age. When Rinko attempts to change the arrangement, she learns a lot about life. The story is set in America during the Great Depression.

1. One reviewer of this book said, "Rinko even at her most pig-headed is immensely likeable." What do you think the reviewer meant by "pig-headed"? Give examples of why one would call Rinko pig-headed.

2. Do you think Rinko should have interfered? Why or why not?

3. What parts of this story give you information about the economic conditions during the 1930s? Make a list and discuss.

Uchida, Yoshiko. **Hisako's Mysteries.** Illustrated by Susan Bennett. Scribner, 1969.

This story, set in Japan in the 1960s, holds several mysteries: Who sent the 1,000-yen note for Hisako's birthday? Who is household helper Hana's artist friend? Why are Grandmother and Grandfather uncomfortable with the mention of Hisako's "dead" father?

1. Thirteen-year-old Hisako is a contrast of behaviors. She is dutiful and respectful but also rambunctious. Write a paragraph describing the type of person you think Hisako is. Would you like her for a friend or not? Why or why not?

2. This story has elements similar to Lillian Eige's *Cady* (HarperCollins, 1987). Compare/contrast that novel with Uchida's story.

Uchida, Yoshiko. **A Jar of Dreams.** McElderry, 1981.

This is the first book in a trilogy that includes *The Best Bad Thing* and *The Happiest Ending*. Eleven-year-old Rinko faces hard times in Berkeley, California, during the Depression (1935). Being Japanese is an added burden for Rinko, who is ridiculed or simply ignored at school. She feels different and left out. She feels like she's a "big nothing."

1. Although part of Rinko's problem is caused by the fact that she is Japanese, other children suffer similar feelings. Many novels for late primary or intermediate readers involve a "problem," and that problem deals with self-esteem and relationships with others. Compare Rinko's story with the relationship involved in a second novel that you read—try any novel by Patricia Reilly Giff, Lois Lowry, Susan Beth Pfeffer, Norma Fox Mazer, Betsy Byars, Katherine Paterson, Paula Danziger, or another favorite novelist.

2. Discuss the way "we" treat people who are somewhat different from ourselves. How are people around us treated as compared to how Rinko was treated? How would you treat Rinko?

Uchida, Yoshiko. **Journey Home.** Illustrated by Charles Robinson. McElderry, 1978.

This is the sequel to *Journey to Topaz: A Story of the Japanese-American Evacuation.* When Yuki's family is released from the Topaz concentration camp, she tries to adjust to a new home. After going first to Salt Lake City, the family settles in Berkeley. Yuki must deal with poor living conditions, prejudice, and the fact that all her family's earthly possessions were lost during their incarceration. She also must deal with her separation from friends and relatives.

1. What evidence of prejudicial behavior is in this story? Discuss alternatives to this type of behavior.

Evidence of Prejudicial Behavior	Suggested New Behavior

2. Do you think Yuki or her family could have done anything differently, something that would have made life easier and more comfortable for them?

Uchida, Yoshiko. **Journey to Topaz: A Story of the Japanese-American Evacuation.** Illustrations by Donald Carrick. Scribner, 1971; Creative Arts, 1985.

During World War II, after the bombing of Pearl Harbor and when the author was 21, she and her family were ordered to live in a horse stall at Tanforan Race Track. They were later sent to Topaz, a concentration camp in the Utah desert. Over 120,000 people of Japanese-American descent were ordered to concentrations camps during the war. This story, told through the eyes of 11-year-old Yuki, is based on the author's family's experiences.

1. Before reading this story, discuss the war, the bombing of Pearl Harbor, and the hysteria that swept across the United States.

2. Read and discuss another book—Hadley Irwin's *Kim/Kimi* (Viking, 1987). Sixteen-year-old Kim needs to find answers about her Japanese-American father, who died before she was born. Kim's search for her father leads her to Sacramento, where she finds some Japanese Americans who are still dealing with the disruption of their lives—a disruption caused by their family's incarceration during World War II.

Uchida, Yoshiko. **The Magic Listening Cap—More Folk Tales from Japan.** Illustrated by Yoshiko Uchida. Harcourt, 1955; reissued Creative Arts, 1987.

The fourteen tales in this collection carry universal themes. The title story, "The Magic Listening Cap," focuses on a poor man who is endowed with the power to understand animals and thus is enabled to save a life and earn a secure future. "The Fox and the Bear" and "The Wrestling Match of the Two Buddhas" are two other stories included in this collection.

1. The following is a list of motifs that are commonly found in folktales.

   - Reoccurring characters: younger brother, wicked stepmother, etc.
   - Magical objects
   - Enchantment
   - Long sleeps
   - Transformations
   - Magical powers
   - Wishes
   - Trickery

   Keeping these motifs in mind, read the tales in this collection and identify the reoccuring themes/motifs. Categorize these tales and other folktales under these themes.

2. Folktales often have the numbers 3 and 7 within the story. Some cultures consider the numbers to be magical. For example, one might attempt to rescue a princess three times, there might be seven animals in the story, a character might be granted three wishes, etc. Identify the times and places the number 3 or 7 appears in each of the stories.

Uchida, Yoshiko. **The Rooster Who Understood Japanese.** Illustrated by Charles Robinson. Scribner, 1976.

Miyo's father is dead and her mother works long hours in a hospital, so Miyo often finds herself in the care of Mrs. Kitamura. Mrs. Kitamura is fond of animals and has several bilingual pets, all named for heroes in American history. When Mrs. Kitamura must give up Mr. Lincoln, a rooster, Miyo finds a new home for him by putting an advertisement in her class newspaper. The story gives a view of a middle-class Japanese-American home.

1. Write an advertisement for another one of Mrs. Kitamura's animals or for another animal. Make it poster size.

2. Miyo's class had a class newspaper. Write a class newspaper for your class. Publish it and take it home at the end of the week. You may wish to put advertisements in your paper.

Uchida, Yoshiko. **Samurai of Gold Hill.** Illustrated by Ati Forberg. Scribner, 1972; reissued Creative Arts, 1985.

A good background in Japanese history will be necessary to fully understand this historical fiction story. Based on the few pieces of information available, the story details life in the ill-fated Wakamatsu Colony, founded at Gold Hill, California. The founders were part of the Japanese clan that was defeated along with the shogun. The 1869 setting, in both Japan and California, is sharply detailed. The story is told from the view of a young boy who must deal with a new life. Koichi has been raised to follow his father as a samurai, but now he must cross the ocean to become a silk and tea farmer. He demonstrates his maturity when he chooses to sell his grandfather's magnificent sword in order to feed the impoverished colony.

1. Research whether or not silk and tea are raised in California today. Does the town of Gold Hill exist?

2. Koichi had been raised to be a samurai. Research what a samurai is.

3. Draw a full-scale representation of the magnificent sword Koichi sold to feed the colony.

Uchida, Yoshiko. **The Sea of Gold, and Other Tales from Japan.** Illustrated by Marianne Yamaguchi. Scribner, 1965.

In the title story in this collection, "The Sea of Gold," the fool is Hikoichi, the cook. Hikoichi, who works on a fishing boat, talks to the fish and feeds them as if they were his friends. The fishermen on the boat mock and tease him. But the fishermen's laughter changes when one night the King of the Sea rewards Hikoichi's kindness a hundredfold. The motif of this tale is the fool who is rewarded for the "foolishness" of kindness, gentleness, and goodness.

1. The motif of the fool/inept character being rewarded for kindness is present in many tales from many cultures. Identify at least two other folktales with a similar motif.

2. Identify the other motifs in the story. Are they similar to those in other tales you have read?

Uchida, Yoshiko. **Sumi and the Goat and the Tokyo Express.** Illustrated by Mizumura. Scribner, 1969. **Sumi's Prize.** Illustrated by Mizumura. Scribner, 1964. **Sumi's Special Happening.** Illustrated by Mizumura. Scribner, 1966.

These three tales are about a young girl, Sumi, in modern (1960) rural Japan. *Sumi's Prize* introduces Sumi and the people of Sugi Village. People are shown wearing a mixture of Japanese and Western clothing, realistic for Japan in the 1960s. The character trait of reverence for the elderly is deftly reflected.

1. These stories are comfortable stories about ordinary happenings in a small village in Japan. Compare the type of activity that occurs in these stories to episodes in stories about other young people in other cultures and settings. The following booklist might be useful. After selecting a title to read, read it and identify the geographical setting and the time period. How do the societies compare?

Ordinary Happenings in Ordinary Places

Barrett, Joyce Durham. *Willie's Not the Hugging Kind*. Illustrated by Pat Cummings. HarperCollins, 1989.

Cooney, Barbara. *Miss Rumphius*. Illustrated by Barbara Cooney. Viking, 1982.

Giff, Patricia Reilly. *I Love Saturday*. Illustrated by Frank Remkiewicz. Viking, 1989.

Jukes, Marvis. *Like Jake and Me*. Illustrated by Lloyd Bloom. Knopf, 1984.

Numeroff, Laura Joffe. *Does Grandma Have an Elmo Elephant Kit?* Greenwillow, 1980.

Rylant, Cynthia. *When I Was Young in the Mountains*. Illustrated by Diane Goode. Dutton, 1982.

Stevens, Carla. *Anna, Grandpa, and the Big Storm*. Illustrated by Margot Tomes. Clarion, 1982.

Stevenson, James. *Emma at the Beach*. Illustrated by James Stevenson. Greenwillow, 1990.

_____. *July*. Illustrated by James Stevenson. Greenwillow, 1990.

Waddell, Martin. *The Hidden House*. Illustrated by Angela Barrett. Philomel, 1990.

Williams, Vera B. *A Chair for My Mother*. Greenwillow, 1982.

Uchida, Yoshiko. **The Two Foolish Cats.** Illustrated by Margot Zemach. McElderry, 1987.

This is a trickster tale from Japan. The two foolish cat hunters, Big Daizo and Little Suki, find no prey, but they do find two rice cakes. Each wants the larger of the rice cakes for himself. In order to settle their quarrel, they take the rice cakes and their argument to the wise old monkey of the mountain. The monkey tricks them out of both cakes and teaches them the lesson of sharing.

1. Discuss the element of trickery in folktales. Then extend the concept by introducing students to some of the following tales of trickery.

Tales of Trickery

Bang, Molly. *Wiley and the Hairy Man*. Illustrated by Molly Bang. Macmillan, 1976.

Berson, Harold. *Balarin's Goat*. Illustrated by Harold Berson. Crown, 1972.

Brown, Marcia. *Stone Soup*. Illustrated by Marcia Brown. Scribner, 1947.

dePaola, Tomie. *Fin M'Coul: The Giant of Knockmany Hill*. Illustrated by Tomie dePaola. Holiday, 1981.

Galdone, Paul. *Puss in Boots*. Illustrated by Paul Galdone. Clarion, 1976.

He Liyi. "Never Heard of This Before." In *The Spring of Butterflies and Other Chinese Folk Tales*. Lothrop, 1986.

Jaquith, Priscilla. *Bo Rabbit Smart for True: Folktales from the Gullah*. Illustrated by Ed Young. Philomel, 1981.

Sherlock, Philip. "Anansi and the Old Hag." In *Anansi the Spider Man: Jamaican Folk Tales*. Illustrated by Marcia Brown. Crowell, 1954.

Singer, Isaac Bashevis. "Shrewd Todie and Lyzer, the Miser." In *When Shlemiel Went to Warsaw and Other Stories*. Translated by Isaac Bashevis Singer and Elizabeth Shub. Illustrated by Margot Zemach. Farrar, 1968.

2. In this story the monkey is portrayed as a trickster. Correlate responses for this story with those suggested for Patricia McKissack's *Monkey-Monkey's Trick: Based on an African Folk Tale* (see index).

FURTHER READING

Daniel Davis's *Behind Barbed Wire: The Imprisonment of Japanese Americans during World War II* (Dutton, 1982) is a nonfiction account of the harsh consequences of war for Japanese Americans. It is written for the intermediate or middle/junior high school reader, but portions might be selectively read aloud with younger students.

Laurence Yep

From *Bookpeople: A Multicultural Album* by Sharron L. McElmeel (Libraries Unlimited, Inc., 1992)

Laurence Yep

Laurence Yep was born June 14, 1948, in San Francisco, California, where he now lives. His Chinese-American family lived in an African-American section of San Francisco, and Laurence commuted to a bilingual school in Chinatown. His father was born in China and came to America when he was 10. His mother had been brought up in West Virginia, where her family for a time was the only Chinese family in the area. In San Francisco the Yep family owned a corner grocery store. One of Laurence's memories of his childhood is of the traditional cookies shaped in the form of a pig. These cookies were part of the Chinese harvest festival. His grandmother often made the treasured cookies, adding sugar to her recipe to please her grandchildren.

As a freshman in college Yep wrote science fiction short stories for magazines for which he was paid 1 cent per word. Several years later a college friend who worked for a publisher asked him to write a science fiction book for children. *Sweetwater* was his first book. His second book, *Dragonwings*, was set in early-twentieth-century San Francisco. His science fiction books include elements from his Chinese heritage. He has also written three mysteries and a "horror" book, *The Curse of the Squirrel*.

Laurence Yep is married to the college friend, Joanne Ryder, who first asked him to write a book. She is also an author. They live in San Francisco.

Laurence Yep

ABOUT THE AUTHOR

Laurence Michael Yep was born June 14, 1948. He grew up in San Francisco, his birthplace, and although both his parents were of Chinese heritage, the family did not live in Chinatown.

Yep's mother, Franché Lee, was the youngest child in her family. She was born in Ohio and raised in Bridgeport, West Virginia, near Clarksburg, where her father opened a Chinese laundry. The Lees were the only Chinese family in the area until another Chinese laundry opened. While the children were still at home, Yep's grandmother packed up the family—which included his mother, his aunts, and his uncle—and returned them to California, where the "girls could meet a nice Chinese man."[1] His grandmother divorced his grandfather and sometimes worked two jobs, as a seamstress and a nanny, in order to support her family.

Yep's father, Thomas Gim Yep, was born in China. He was almost abandoned because the family had enough boys. When he was 10, the family brought him to America, where they lived in a white neighborhood with an Irish friend of his father's father. His father and his Irish friend lost everything during the Great Depression, but eventually Thomas Yep was able to open a grocery store—in a predominantly African-American neighborhood. The grocery story reflected his father's frustration—he had always wanted to be a chemist or a television repairman.

Yep's parents met in San Francisco and settled in an apartment above the grocery store. Yep felt like an alien, an outsider; he was the all-purpose Asian. When he and his friends played war, he was the Japanese who got killed. When the Korean War came, he was the North Korean communist. Yep attended a parochial bilingual school in San Francisco's Chinatown, where many of the students spoke both Chinese and English. Yep, however, spoke only English, so he was put in "the dumbbell Chinese class." His first confrontation with "white American culture" came when he attended high school. His grammar school friends "went into basketball"; it was during his high school years that Yep became acquainted with science fiction and other forms of literature—from great novels to children's literature to comic books. He began to write science fiction short stories, and by the time he was 18 and a freshman at Marquette University, he was a published writer. He wrote for science fiction magazines and was paid 1 cent per word.

At Marquette Yep met Joanne Ryder, editor of a campus newspaper; he was art editor. He transferred to the University of California at Santa Cruz and from there went to the State University of New York at Buffalo, where, in 1975, he earned his Ph.D in English. His dissertation examined William Faulkner's work. After he had his doctorate, he sent out 500 job applications but was unable to secure a position at a university. So he taught at a junior college and at satellite campuses. While teaching he "learned students did not have a sense of [their own] history."

By this time, his friend Joanne Ryder was working as special assistant to Ursula Nordstrom, an editor at Harper & Row (now HarperCollins). She asked Yep to try writing a science fiction book for younger readers. He did, and the result was his first book, *Sweetwater*. It is the story of Tyree, who is a descendant of the first colonists, from Earth, to inhabit the star Harmony. When he finished the book, he thought about the aliens he had created and thought that in some ways those aliens, the Argans, were like the Chinese—new settlers to a foreign land. His next book, *Dragonwings*, was the first in which he examined his own heritage. The story, set in early-twentieth-century San Francisco, evolved from some of Yep's research on Fong Joe Guey, a Chinese man who built and flew an airplane in the Oakland hills in 1909. Yep was doing some general Chinese-American research, he was trying to locate information about people of Chinese ancestry who were influenced by their experiences in America. Yep conducted research for 6 years

---

[1] Laurence Yep, presentation at the International Reading Association Convention, May 8, 1990, Atlanta, Georgia.

but found only bits and pieces. Many of the Chinese who came were men who could not afford or who did not qualify (by U.S. immigration law) to send for their wives and families. As a result much of the Chinese community was a bachelor society. When the men grew old they sent for their sons, or other male relatives, to take their place. These men did not see their loved ones for 5 or 10 years at a time. Eventually, in 1965, the laws were relaxed. The Chinese chose to push away memories of these bachelor societies and the past discrimination. So, while keeping a distance between themselves and white Americans, the Chinese Americans chose to imitate elements of the white culture within their Chinatown setting rather than join into the outside culture. Third-generation Chinese Americans, like Yep, often do not speak Chinese and are ignorant of the rich Chinese myths and legends of their heritage.

It was a record of his ancestors that Yep was researching when his notes revealed the story of Fong Joe Guey. In 1909 Guey actually built and flew a flying machine for 20 minutes. The flight itself was not difficult to write about, but events that preceded or followed the flight were difficult to document, so he used the flight as fact but fictionalized the aviator. He became Windrider. The story is told through the words of his son Young Moon Shadow, who has come to California; both are part of the bachelor society. Yep's own father is part of both characters — father and son.

Yep remembers savoring the times when, as a child, he would receive a special pig-shaped cookie during the Chinese harvest festival. The cookies were in a cage tied with a red ribbon. At the appointed time, the cage would be untied and the pigs freed and eaten. When Yep returned to Chinatown and to the bakery he remembered as a child, the pig cookies were not there. So, for a few years he inquired at bakeries he thought might still offer his childhood treat and was finally successful. He had a special feeling about the cookies, because his grandmother had often made them for him and her other grandchildren — a special version with sugar.

This grandmother was tough and independent. When she was 70 she had a boyfriend, Mr. Wang, who was 60. He wanted to get married, but she didn't want to get too involved. Her life was a contrast of things Chinese and American. At night the radio was tuned to a Chinese station, but during the day it blared rock music. In one of his books, *Child of the Owl*, Yep includes memories of his grandmother. The story is set in the Chinatown of the 1960s. Casey, a Chinese American, faces her ethnic heritage when she stays with her grandmother in Chinatown.

Sea Glass focuses on Craig Chin, an eighth grader who moves to a suburban community and misses his old neighborhood and friends. Yep says that *Sea Glass* is the most autobiographical of all of his books. Then, departing from his emphasis on cultural heritage, Yep wrote a romance, *Kind Hearts and Gentle Monsters*, and two more science fiction books, *Dragon of the Lost Sea* and *Dragon Steel*. He returned to his cultural emphasis with *The Serpent's Children* and *Mountain Light*. He has also written three mysteries: *The Mark Twain Murders, Liar, Liar,* and *The Tom Sawyer Fires*. His Stepping Stone Book, *The Curse of the Squirrel*, is a book designed for intermediate readers who need easier reading material. In *The Curse of the Squirrel*, in a section about the author, Yep is quoted as saying, "I've always been a fan of classic horror movies — though I would be scared for days after seeing one. In *The Curse of the Squirrel* I finally achieved an old ambition to write a horror story of my own. But instead of being frightened, I got to laugh a lot."

Laurence Yep married his college friend Joanne Ryder, who is a children's book author. Some of her books are *Inside Turtle's Shell and Other Poems of the Field* (Macmillan, 1985), *The Night Flight* (Four Winds, 1985), and *Step into the Night* (Four Winds, 1988). She dedicated *Hello, Tree!* (Lodestar, 1991), a poetic celebration of nature, to Franché Yep and to the memory of Thomas Gim Yep. Yep lived for a time in Sunnyvale, California, where his mother still lives, but now spends much of the year in San Francisco.

THE BOOKSHELF

Yep, Laurence. **Child of the Owl.** HarperCollins, 1977.

Twelve-year-old Casey discovers her heritage through Chinese folklore and history. The story is set in the smaller, quieter Chinatown of the 1950s, where Casey goes to stay with her grandmother when her compulsive gambler father is hospitalized.

1. In October 1965, the immigration laws were made fairer and more Asians could enter the United States. The law changed Chinatown in both geography and population. Other programs such as Medicare and upgraded housing standards also contributed to the change. Find out what you can about Chinatown today and the Chinatown of the 1950s (the setting of the book). Possible research methods include:

    a. Newspapers from the San Francisco area in the 1950s and current papers.

    b. Letters of inquiry to the San Francisco Chamber of Commerce.

    c. Encyclopedias. (Be sure to check the copyright date to establish the period of time for the specific information.)

    d. Books about San Francisco. (Use the index of the books to locate the sections on Chinatown. Check the copyright date.)

2. Compare how Casey changed from the beginning of the story to the end of the story.

3. Compare Casey's grandmother to your own grandmother or an older member of your family. Are there any similarities? Differences? Do you think the similarities and differences are due to cultural differences or to personalities?

Yep, Laurence. **The Curse of the Squirrel.** Illustrated by Dirk Zimmer. Random, 1987. (Stepping Stone Book)

Farmer Johnson and his two hunting dogs are frightened by the giant squirrel who stalks the woods. At first Howie the hound does not believe his brother, Willie. But soon they learn about the curse of the squirrel.

1. Discuss what the curse of the squirrel was. Do you really think it was a curse for the dog?

2. How is this story like *The Whingdingdilly* by Bill Peet (Houghton, 1970)?

3. After reading other stories with a squirrel character, discuss how the squirrel is portrayed in fiction.

Squirrels in Books

Ashabranner, Brent. *I'm in the Zoo, Too!* Illustrated by Janet Stevens. Cobblehill, 1989.

Collins, Pat Lowry. *Tomorrow, Up and Away!* Illustrated by Lynn Munsinger. Houghton, 1990.

Peet, Bill. *Merle the High Flying Squirrel.* Illustrated by Bill Peet. Houghton, 1974.

Potter, Beatrix. *The Story of Squirrel Nutkin.* Illustrated by Beatrix Potter. Warne, 1903.

Sharmat, Marjorie Weinman. *Sophie and Gussie.* Illustrated by Lillian Hoban. Macmillan, 1973.

Stevenson, James. *Wilfred the Rat.* Illustrated by James Stevenson. Greenwillow, 1977.

Zion, Gene. *The Meanest Squirrel I Ever Met.* Illustrated by Margaret Blay Graham. Scribner, 1962.

Yep, Laurence. **Dragon of the Lost Sea.** HarperCollins, 1982. **Dragon Steel.** HarperCollins, 1985.

In *Dragon of the Lost Sea*, a fantasy quest based on Chinese myths, the exiled dragon princess, Shimmer, feels that humans are beneath her notice. But she allows young Thorn to join her in the search for the evil witch Civet. The princess is on a quest to restore her dragon clan's lost home. In *Dragon Steel*, the continuation of *Dragon of the Lost Sea*, Shimmer and Thorn return to her underwater kingdom thinking that they will be rewarded by the High King for capturing Civet. Instead, they find that they must continue their quest in order to restore the dragon clan to its ancestral throne. This story has dungeons, sea monsters, and magicians.

1. Expand students' understanding of the quest tale by having them read other tales with a quest theme.

Stories of Quest

Cole, Brock. *The Goats.* Farrar, 1987.

George, Jean Craighead. *Julie of the Wolves.* HarperCollins, 1972.

Hamilton, Virginia. *M. C. Higgins the Great.* Macmillan, 1974.

Paulsen, Gary. *Dogsong.* Bradbury, 1985.

Voigt, Cynthia. *Homecoming.* Atheneum, 1981.

_____. *Dicey's Song.* Atheneum, 1982.

2. Suggest that students make a poster advertising one of these books to other science fiction fans.

3. List/discuss with students which elements of the story came from the Chinese tradition.

Yep, Laurence. **Dragonwings.** HarperCollins, 1975.

Windrider and his son, Moon Shadow, build a flying machine in this historical novel set in early-twentieth-century San Francisco. The father and son are part of the Chinese bachelor society that existed during this period. The story is based on an actual event that took place in 1909 (September 23). One of the episodes includes a description of the earthquake from an immigrant's viewpoint. American School Publishers has this title available in filmstrip/cassette format.

1. During a study of natural disasters, read the section in Yep's book describing the 1906 earthquake and correlate that description with information in books specifically about earthquakes.

Earthquakes

Branley, Franklyn M. *Earthquakes.* Illustrated by Richard Rosenblum. Crowell, 1990.

Elting, Mary. *Volcanoes and Earthquakes.* Illustrated by Courtney. Simon, 1990.

Yep, Laurence. **Kind Hearts and Gentle Monsters.** HarperCollins, 1982.

In this romance for the older reader, Charley Sabini is a high school sophomore who feels that logic and reason are always on his side. Chris Pomeroy doesn't need logical reasoning for anything, and when she reenters Charley's life, they both find themselves in a unique romance.

1. Compare and contrast Charley and Chris with Motown and Didi from Walter Dean Myers's *Motown and Didi: A Love Story.*

2. Make a comparison chart (see appendix A) comparing Charley and Chris.

3. How did Charley and Chris's relationship change each of them? Compare Charley's character at the beginning of the story to the person he is at the end of the story. Make the same comparison for Chris.

4. Describe the setting of this story, and then list ten ways that the setting is the same as or different from the area where you live.

5. Extend the theme of friendship and love by reading one of the books on the following booklist: compare and contrast it with Yep's title.

Friendship and Love

DeClements, Barthe. *How Do You Lose Those Ninth Grade Blues?* Viking, 1983.

_____. *Seventeen & In-Between.* Viking, 1984.

Gay, Rosa. *My Love, My Love, or the Peasant Girl.* Holt, 1985.

Hamilton, Virginia. *A Little Love.* Putnam, 1984.

Kerr, M. E. *Little Little.* Harper, 1981.

McDonnell, Christine. *Friends First.* Viking, 1990.

McKinley, Robin. *The Blue Sword.* Greenwillow, 1982.

Myers, Walter Dean. *Motown and Didi: A Love Story.* Viking, 1984.

Newton, Suzanne. *M. V. Sexton Speaking.* Viking, 1981.

Pevsner, Stella. *I'll Always Remember You ... Maybe.* Clarion, 1981.

Wilhelm, Kate. *Oh, Susannah!* Houghton, 1982.

Yep, Laurence. **Liar, Liar.** Morrow, 1983; Avon, 1985.

In an instant the car is a ball of fire, and Sean Pierce's best friend, Marsh, is dead. The police write the accident off to a teenage driver with a battered old heap with faulty brakes. But Sean doesn't believe it was an accident. He suspects that Marsh played one practical joke too many, and that the joke cost him his life. But nobody wants to believe Sean's accusations. Sean has a reputation for lying—even his friends and family don't believe his story about the stranger who rigged the brakes to kill Marsh. Sean has to prove there has been a murder—and prove it before he becomes the next victim.

1. This mystery is excitement enough. But those who need another book just as exciting should try one of the following.

Mysteries Too Good to Miss

Corbett, Scott. *Grave Doubts.* Little, Brown, 1982.

Ferguson, Alane. *Show Me the Evidence.* Avon, 1989.

Hamilton, Virginia. *The House of Dies Drear.* Illustrated by Eros Keith. Macmillan, 1968.

2. Have students locate more mystery books by using the subject heading MYSTERY AND DETECTIVE STORIES.

Yep, Laurence. **The Mark Twain Murders.** Four Winds, 1982.

This story is told from the viewpoint of an urchin who calls himself "His Grace the Duke of Baywater." A young Mark Twain, who has a less-than-successful reputation as a reporter, gets in the way of Twain's efforts to get to the bottom of a San Francisco murder.

1. Was the writer Mark Twain an important element in this story, or could the book and character have been given any other name, such as *The Aubrey Jade Murders?* Would the story have been the same had the character been Aubrey Jade instead of Mark Twain? If using the name and title Mark Twain was important, explain why. If you think it wasn't important, explain why Yep used that name and title.

2. Read the other mysteries by Laurence Yep: *Liar, Liar* (Morrow, 1983) and *The Tom Sawyer Fires* (Morrow, 1984). See annotation above for *Liar, Liar.*

Yep, Laurence. **Mountain Light.** HarperCollins, 1985. **The Serpent's Children.** HarperCollins, 1984.

The first book in these companion titles is *The Serpent's Children*. Cassia fights famine, bandits, and poverty while her widowed father tries to teach her and her brother to help free China from both Manchu and foreign domination. The story is set against the backdrop of the nineteenth-century Chinese Taiping Rebellion in Kwangtung Province. In *Mountain Light*, Squeaky Lau falls in love with the independent Cassia during their flight after an unsuccessful rebellion against the Manchus. Despite his love for Cassia, he leaves China to make his fortune in California. The setting is China and California in 1855.

1. Use an encyclopedia to locate some background information about Manchu and the Taiping Rebellion. Be sure to use the index of the encyclopedia to access all the references to Manchu and the rebellion.

2. Make a list of characteristics of China and of California in 1855. What differences could a traveler expect to find between those two places in the mid-1800s?

3. Focus on the setting of this story and compare China of 1855 with China today. Make the same comparison with California. Present the information by

   a. writing a fictionalized account of a person who wakes up in the twentieth century either in China or California after having been asleep for over a century;

   b. creating 1855 travel brochures for China and California;

   c. making a poster to post in China advertising the reasons one would want to emigrate to California.

Yep, Laurence. **Sea Glass.** HarperCollins, 1979.

Craig Chin is an eighth grader. His parents are first-generation Chinese Americans. The family moves from their Chinatown home to the suburbs, but Craig misses his old neighborhood and finds his cousins' insults about his weight, his athletic ability, and his acknowledgment of his Chinese heritage almost unbearable.

1. Yep has said that this book is his most autobiographical. After sharing with students information about Yep and his background, discuss with them similarities between the young Yep and Craig Chin. For example, Craig "wheeled piles of boxes into the store on a creaky hand truck." This is a task Yep performed in his father's grocery store.

2. Yep often felt like an outsider in his school: he didn't speak Chinese, he wasn't athletic, he liked to read—and write—and he was a bit chubby. Would this characterization of Yep be similar to how you would characterize Craig?

3. Compare Craig Chin's experiences when he moved to a new neighborhood with Felita's in Nicholasa Mohr's *Felita* (see index).

FURTHER READING

Laurence Yep is a Chinese American who has written many books for the intermediate or middle-school reader. Most of his novels reflect elements from his Chinese heritage, although he has written some books that do not focus on the Chinese experience. There are few Chinese or Chinese Americans who write for children and young adults. Although most of Yep's novels are for the more able intermediate reader, they can be used with a younger group or class by reading aloud portions or chapters of the books. In conjunction with reading his books, discuss Laurence Yep's heritage — the background of his parents and his own growing-up years. American School Publishers combine information about the author's background with summaries of Yep's novels in their filmstrip/casssette *Meet the Newbery Author: Laurence Yep.* The immigration theme could be extended into the social studies curriculum. Suggestions for more reading on this theme are given at the end of the chapter featuring Nicholasa Mohr (see index).

Demi is an author/illustrator who has become interested in Chinese culture. She has studied Chinese art forms and stories and has told several tales that come from the Chinese tradition. Some books by Demi to introduce to students are *Paintbrush* (Holt, 1980), *The Artist and the Architect* (Holt, 1991), *The Magic Boat* (Holt, 1990), and *The Empty Pot* (Holt, 1990).

Appendix A

Reproducibles

CHARACTER WEB

In the oval in the center of the web, place the character's name. In each of the rectangles place a character trait that could be attributed to the character for whom the web is being created. On the lines below each trait, cite sources and page numbers of excerpts from stories that would substantiate the validity of the trait attributed to the character.

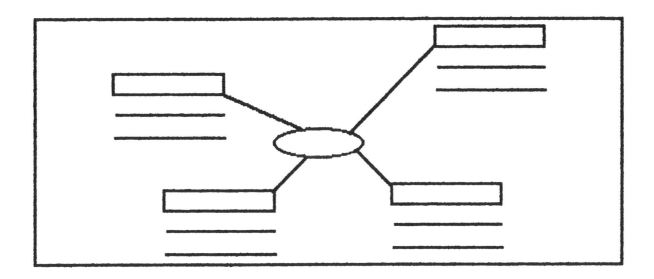

COMPARISON CHART

Title/Character A

Both A/B

Title/Character B

PLOTTING STORY GRAMMAR

A Story Map

for _____ by _____
(Story title)   (author/illustrator name)

Setting/time	Main characters

Problem _____
_____
_____

First attempt to resolve the problem _____
_____
_____

Second attempt to resolve the problem _____
_____
_____

Third attempt to resolve the problem _____
_____
_____

Resolution/problem solved _____
_____
_____

Conclusion/climax _____
_____
_____

Appendix B

Addresses of Authors/Illustrators
and Publishers

ADDRESSES OF AUTHORS/ILLUSTRATORS

Since some authors' personal addresses may change, it is recommended that you send correspondence in care of the Children's Book Marketing Division of the author's most recent publisher. Address an envelope to the publisher, enclose your letter to the author in a stamped envelope, and insert a memo requesting the publisher to forward the letter to the author.

Mitsumasa Anno
Anno requests that his address not be published.
He lives in Tokyo, Japan.

Ashley Bryan
Islesford, Maine 04646
or Ashley Bryan (author)
c/o Macmillan Children's Book Group
866 Third Avenue, 25th Floor
New York, NY 10022

Ann Cameron
Panajachel, 07010 Sololá
Guatemala, Central America

Donald Crews
653 Carroll Street
Brooklyn, NY 11215
or Donald Crews (author)
c/o Greenwillow Books
105 Madison Avenue
New York, NY 10016

Pat Cummings (author)
c/o HarperCollins Publishers—Children's Books
10 East 53rd Street,
New York, NY 10022

Mem Fox
Fox requests that her address not be published.
She lives in Adelaide, Australia.

Paul Goble
P.O. Box 1239
Lewiston, NY 14092

Jamake Highwater (author)
c/o Dial Books for Young Readers
375 Hudson St.
New York, NY 10016

Julius Lester
Box 333
North Amherst, MA 01059-0333

Patricia McKissack
c/o All-Writing Services
225 South Meramec #506
St. Louis, MO 63105

Nicholasa Mohr
727 President Street
Brooklyn, NY 11215
or Nicholasa Mohr (author)
Bantam Doubleday Dell Publishing Group, Inc.
Attn: Children's Books Publicity
666 Fifth Avenue, 24th Floor
New York, NY 10103

Brian Pinkney
444 Henry Street
Brooklyn, NY 11231

Virginia Driving Hawk Sneve
723 Wright Court,
Rapid City, SD 57701

Yoshiko Uchida
1685 Solano Avenue #102,
Berkeley, CA 94707
or Yoshiko Uchida (author),
c/o Margaret K. McElderry Books
866 Third Avenue
New York, NY 10022

Laurence Yep
593 Eleventh Avenue
San Francisco, CA 94118

ADDRESSES OF SELECTED PUBLISHERS
AND OTHER SOURCES

Note: Publishers' addresses may change. For complete and up-to-date information, see the current edition of *Literary Market Place* or *Children's Books in Print*.

Aladdin Books. See Macmillan Children's Books.

Albert Whitman & Co., 6340 Oakton Street, Morton Grove, IL 60053

American School Publishers, Princeton Road, Box 408, Hightstown, NY 08520-9377

Arte Público Press, Division of University of Houston, 4800 Calhoun Street, Houston, TX 77204

Atheneum Books for Children, 866 Third Avenue, New York, NY 10022

Avon Books, 105 Madison Avenue, New York, NY 10022

Ballantine Books, 201 East 50th Street, New York, NY 10016

Bantam Books. See Bantam Doubleday Dell Publishing Group, Inc.

Bantam Doubleday Dell Publishing Group, Inc., Attn: Children's Books Publicity, 666 Fifth Avenue, New York, NY 10103

Bradbury Press, 866 Third Avenue, New York, NY 10022

Carolrhoda Books. See Lerner Publications.

Charles Scribner's Sons, 866 Third Avenue, New York, NY 10022

Charlesbridge Publishing, 85 Main Street, Watertown, MA 02172

Children's Press, 5440 North Cumberland Avenue, Chicago, IL 60656

Clarion Books, 52 Vanderbilt Avenue, New York, NY 10017

Collier Books. See Aladdin Books.

Creative Arts Book Co., 833 Bancroft Way, Berkeley, CA 94710

Dell Publishing. See Bantam Doubleday Dell Publishing Group, Inc.

Dial Books for Young Readers, 375 Hudson Street, New York, NY 10014

Doubleday Publishing. See Bantam Doubleday Dell Publishing Group.

Dutton Children's Books, 375 Hudson Street, New York, NY 10014

Farrar, Straus & Giroux, 19 Union Square West, New York, NY 10003

Four Winds Press, 866 Third Avenue, New York, NY 10022

Franklin Watts, Inc., 387 Park Avenue South, New York, NY 10016

Frederick Warne & Co., 375 Hudson Street, New York, NY 10014

Gareth Stevens Children's Books, 1555 N. Rivercenter Drive, Rivercenter Building, Suite 201, Milwaukee, WI 53212

Great Plains National Instructional Television Library, P.O. Box 80669, Lincoln, NE 68501

Green Tiger Press, 1230 Avenue of the Americas, New York, NY 10020

Greenwillow Books, 105 Madison Avenue, New York, NY 10016

Harcourt Brace Jovanovich Children's Book Division, 1250 Sixth Avenue, San Diego, CA 92101

HarperCollins Children's Books, 10 East 53rd Street, New York, NY 10022

Harry N. Abrams, Inc., 100 Fifth Avenue, New York, NY 10011

Henry Holt and Co., 115 West 18th Street, New York, NY 10011

Holiday House Inc., 425 Madison Avenue, New York, NY 10017

Holt, Rinehart & Winston, Inc., 111 Fifth Avenue, New York, NY 10003

Julian Messner, a division of Simon & Schuster, Inc. See Simon & Schuster, Inc.

Kane-Miller Publishing, P.O. Box 529, Brooklyn, NY 11231

Kidstamps, P.O. Box 18699, Cleveland Heights, OH 44118

Lerner Publications, 241 First Avenue North, Minneapolis, MN 55401

Little, Brown and Co., 334 Beacon Street, Boston, MA 02108

Live Oak Media, P.O. Box 34, Ancramdale, NY 12503

Lodestar Books, 375 Hudson Street, New York, NY 10014

Lothrop, Lee & Shepard Books, 105 Madison Avenue, New York, NY 10016

Macmillan Children's Books, 866 Third Avenue, New York, NY 10022

Margaret K. McElderry Books, 866 Third Avenue, New York, NY 10022

McElderry Books. See Margaret K. McElderry Books.

Merrill Publishing Company, Columbus, Ohio 43216

Orchard Books, 387 Park Avenue South, New York, NY 10016

Penguin Books—Australia, P.O. Box 257, Ringwood 3134, Australia

Penguin USA, 375 Hudson Street, New York, NY 10014

Picture Book Studio, 10 Central Street, Saxoonville, MA 01701

Pied Piper/Dial Books for Young Readers. See Penguin USA.

Puffin Books, 375 Hudson Street, New York, NY 10014

Putnam & Grosset Book Group, 200 Madison Avenue, New York, NY 10016

Random House, Inc., 225 Park Avenue South, New York, NY 10003

Scholastic Inc., 730 Broadway, New York, NY 10003

Scribner. See Charles Scribner's Sons.

Silver Burdett Press, 190 Sylvan Avenue, Englewood Cliffs, NJ 07632

Simon & Schuster, Inc., Simon & Schuster Building, Rockefeller Center, 1230 Avenue of the Americas, New York, NY 10020

Tom Snyder Productions, Inc., 90 Sherman Street, Cambridge, MA 02140

Trumpet Books, 666 Fifth Avenue, New York, NY 10103

Viking Children's Books, 375 Hudson Street, New York, NY 10014

Walker & Co., 720 Fifth Avenue, New York, NY 10019

Warne. See Frederick Warne & Co.

Warner Books, 666 Fifth Avenue, New York, NY 10103

Watts. See Franklin Watts, Inc.

Weston Woods, Weston, CT 06883

Whitman. See Albert Whitman & Co.

William Morrow & Co., Inc., 105 Madison Avenue, New York, NY 10016

Appendix C

Photograph Credits

PHOTOGRAPH CREDITS

Photograph of Mitsumasa Anno courtesy of Mitsumasa Anno.

Photograph of Ashley Bryan by Sharron McElmeel.

Photograph of Ann Cameron by Das Anudas. Reprinted by permission of Random House, Inc.

Photograph of Donald Crews by Sharron McElmeel.

Photograph of Donald Crews and Ann Jonas by Sharron McElmeel.

Art from *Truck* © 1980 by Donald Crews, reproduced by permission of Viking Penguin, a division of Penguin USA.

Art from *Freight Train* © 1978 by Donald Crews, reproduced by permission of Viking Penguin, a division of Penguin USA.

Photograph of Pat Cummings by Percidia, reproduced by permission of HarperCollins Publishers.

Book jacket art for *Willie's Not the Hugging Kind* by Joyce Durham.

Barrett, book jacket illustration © 1989 by Pat Cummings, reproduced courtesy of Harper-Collins Publishers.

Book jacket art for *Storm in the Night* by Mary Stolz, book jacket illustration © 1988 by Pat Cummings, reproduced courtesy of HarperCollins Publishers.

Book jacket art for *Just Us Women* by Jeannette Caines, book jacket illustration © 1982 by Pat Cummings, reproduced courtesy of HarperCollins Publishers.

Photograph of Mem Fox and her "fox" courtesy of Mem Fox and reproduced with her permission.

Photograph of Mem Fox by Colin Lambert and reproduced by permission of Harcourt Brace Jovanovich.

Book jacket art for *Koala Lou* by Mem Fox, jacket art © 1988 by Pamela Lofts, reproduced by permission of Harcourt Brace Jovanovich.

Book jacket art for *Night Noises* by Mem Fox, jacket art © 1989 by Terry Denton, reproduced by permission of Harcourt Brace Jovanovich.

Book jacket art for *Possum Magic* by Mem Fox, jacket art © 1983 by Julie Vivas, reproduced by permission of Harcourt Brace Jovanovich.

Photograph of Paul Goble by Janet Goble. Reprinted courtesy of Paul Goble and Bradbury Press, an affiliate of the Macmillan Children's Book Group.

Photograph of Jamake Highwater by Sharron McElmeel.

Photograph of Julius Lester reproduced by permission of Scholastic, Inc.

Photograph of Patricia McKissack by Sharron McElmeel.

Photograph of Nicholasa Mohr by Cindy Grossman courtesy of Arte Público Press and reproduced with permission.

Book jacket art for *Going Home* by Nicholasa Mohr; jacket art for Bantam-Skylark/Dell edition by Rick Mujica reproduced courtesy of Bantam Books.

Book jacket art for *Felita* by Nicholasa Mohr; jacket art for Bantam-Skylark/Dell edition by Rick Mujica reproduced courtesy of Bantam Books.

Photograph of Brian Pinkney by Andrea R. Davis courtesy of Brian Pinkney and reproduced with permission.

Art work from *The Boy and the Ghost* by Robert D. San Souci © 1989 by Brian Pinkney and reproduced with permission.

Art work from *Where Does the Trail Lead?* by Burton Albert, © 1991 by Brian Pinkney and reproduced with permission.

Photography of Virginia Driving Hawk Sneve courtesy of Virginia Driving Hawk Sneve and reproduced with permission.

Photograph of Yoshiko Uchida by Deborah Storms courtesy of Yoshiko Uchida and reproduced with permission.

Photograph of Laurence Yep by Sharron McElmeel.

Bookpeople/An Author a Month Cumulative Index

Bookpeople: A First Album and *Bookpeople: A Second Album* showcased over eighty authors and illustrators in capsule units. This book, *Bookpeople: A Multicultural Album*, adds an additional fifteen authors and illustrators to that list. *An Author a Month (for Pennies)* and *An Author a Month (for Nickels)* showcased an additional twenty-four authors/illustrators. The cumulative index that follows will direct the user to the publication that includes the unit for each of the authors and illustrators covered in the five publications. The following list provides the code for each publication.

A—*An Author a Month (for Pennies)* (Libraries Unlimited, 1988)

N—*An Author a Month (for Nickels)* (Libraries Unlimited, 1990)

F—*Bookpeople: A First Album* (Libraries Unlimited, 1990)

MC—*Bookpeople: A Multicultural Album* (Libraries Unlimited, 1992)

S—*Bookpeople: A Second Album* (Libraries Unlimited, 1990)

Index

About the Author

In addition to authoring seven reference books for educators, Sharron McElmeel has maintained her role as professional educator, parent, grandparent, book reviewer, and educational consultant. She frequently speaks with educators and parents sharing strategies and tested ideas in the area of integration, whole language, and in particular the infusion of literature-based activities across the curriculum. She earned a B.A. in Education from the University of Northern Iowa; M.A. in Library Science from the University of Iowa; and has completed post-graduate work in the area of school administration, reading, and library science. Her experience includes classroom and library media center assignments, both elementary and secondary. She currently is a library media specialist in a K-5 school in the Cedar Rapids (Iowa) Community School District.

She is a contributing editor and columnist for *Iowa Reading Journal* and reviews books/nonprint materials for two professional reviewing journals. Her columns on authors and books are regular features in *Mystery Scene Magazine* and the *Iowa Reading Newspaper*. She lectures and conducts inservice sessions and teaches college courses in children's and young adult literature and in reading. In 1987 she was named Iowa Reading Teacher of the Year.

Her previous books include: *An Author a Month (for Pennies)*; *An Author a Month (for Nickels)*; *Bookpeople: A First Album*; *Bookpeople: A Second Album*; *My Bag of Book Tricks*; and *Adventures with Social Studies (through Literature)*.

She lives with her husband in a rural area north of Cedar Rapids, Iowa, where, at various times, they have shared their home with six children, grandchildren, a dog, two cats (actually the animals share the garage), and several hundred books.